Tom and Jutta

Tom and Jutta

A Jewish Boy of Hungary
An Aryan Girl of Germany

The Story of Tom and Jutta Gerendas

as told to
Barbara W. Pless

The events, locations, and conversations in this book, while true, are recreated from the subjects' memory. However, the essence of the story, and the feelings and emotions evoked, are intended to be accurate representations. In certain instances names have been changed to protect an individual's privacy.

For further information: tomandjuttastory@gmail.com

Library of Congress Control Number: 2018913135

ISBN-13: 978-1-7329264-0-0
Barbara Pless, First Print-On-Demand Edition: November, 2018

eISBN-13: 978-1-7329264-1-7
Barbara Pless, First Electronic Edition: November, 2018

Cover watercolor: Martha Waite
Cover graphics: Deborah Pless
Digitizing: Barry Kaplan at The Finer Image, Danvers, MA
Website design: Greg van Ermen, David Orr
Author photo: Suzanne Hodson

Dedication

To all those who provided for Tom and Jutta
as they navigated the challenges
of their growing years.

Table of Contents

1	Tom	Summer 1947 Budapest, Hungary	23
2	Tom	1932-1940 Budapest	27
3	Tom	1940-1941 Budapest	41
4	Tom	Spring 1944 Budapest	47
5	Tom	Summer 1944 Budapest	53
6	Tom	Fall 1944 Budapest	61
7	Tom	Fall 1944 Budapest	71
8	Tom	December 1944 Budapest	85
9	Tom	January 1945 Budapest	91
10	Jutta	January 15, 1945 Puschkau, Poland	101
11	Jutta	August-December 1944 Puschkau and Posen, Poland	107
12	Jutta	January 1945 Puschkau and Posen, Poland Czechoslovakia	113
13	Jutta	January-February 1945 Dresden, Germany	119

14	Jutta	February 1945 Aue, Germany	123
15	Jutta	March 1945 Bregenz, Austria	125
16	Jutta	April 1945 Schwartzenberg, Austria	127
17	Jutta	1936-1942 Berlin, Germany	129
18	Jutta	May-August 1945 Dikach, Austria	135
19	Jutta	September 1945-Spring 1946 Oberstaufen, Germany	141
20	Jutta	1942-1945 Wartegau, Poland	145
21	Jutta	Winter 1945-1946 Oberstaufen, Germany	151
22	Jutta	1942-1943 Wartegau, Poland	153
23	Jutta	Spring 1946 Rheden, Germany	157
24	Tom	Winter-Summer 1945 Budpest and Oros, Hungary	159
25	Tom	1946-1950 Budapest	175
26	Jutta	1946-1950 Marienhagen, Germany	185

27	Tom	1950-1954 Budapest	199
28	Tom	1950-1954 Rural Hungary	203
29	Jutta	1950-1956 Wilhelmshaven, Germany	209
30	Tom	1954-1956 Budapest	215
31	Jutta	1956-1957 Lüneburg, Germany	219
32	Jutta	1957-1959 Mülheim, Germany	225
33	Tom	October 1956 Budapest	231
34	Tom	November 1956 Budapest to the Austrian Border	241
35	Tom	November 1956-January 1957 Vienna, Austria	251
36	Tom	January 1957 Vienna, Austria to Halifax, Canada	263
37	Tom	1957-1960 Canada	279
38	Tom	1960 Montreal, Canada	301
39	Jutta	Early September 1959 Germany to Canada	313
40	Jutta	Late September 1959-Spring 1961	317

		Montreal, Canada	
41	Jutta	June 1961 In the Laurentian Mountains	329
42	Tom	June 1961 In the Laurentian Mountains	333
43	Jutta	1961-1962 Montreal	337
44	Tom	1961-1962 Montreal	341
45	Jutta	Summer 1962 Schroon Lake, New York Montreal, Canada	345
46	Tom	1962-1963 Montreal	349
47	Jutta	April 1963 Montreal	353
48	Tom	April 27, 1963 Montreal	355
49	Tom	April 27-May 5, 1963 New York, New England, and Back to Montreal	359
50	Author's Epilogue	April 1963-January 2018	368
	Jutta	Where In Life Do You Stand	371
	Website		373
	Author		375

Acknowledgements

Thanks

- To Gordon and Jane Hugenberger for connecting me with Tom and Jutta and then with Esther.
- To Esther Gerendas Briggs for taking me into her heart and sharing her family's treasured stories. Her skill at transcribing our interviews was invaluable. I would not have been able to proceed without her partnership every step of the way.
- For the support of the family — Rebecca Gerendas Hansen, Maria Gerendas O'Laughlin, Gregg Hansen – who trusted me with their parents' story.
- To my team of editors: Ann Lynch, Deborah Pless, and Susannah Ketchum Glass. The book would not be presentable without them.
- To Martha Waite who blessed us with her skill in painting the watercolor for the cover.
- To Walter and Toni Kim, Kris Perkins, Chris Sherwood, and other past and present ministers at Park Street Church who were friends of Tom and Jutta and who encouraged me in getting their story written down.
- For many friends at Park Street Church and around the world who prayed for me and expressed their eagerness to read the finished book.
- For the encouragement of the many acquaintances, including doctors, nurses, staff at the coffee shops I frequented, who asked me about my work. After a brief sketch of Tom and Jutta's lives, they spoke of their eagerness to read the finished book.
- For the support of my family, Alex, Kerstin, Debbi, and Dan whose prayers and encouragement were invaluable.

And especially to Tom and Jutta for trusting me with their stories.

Introduction

I HEARD ABOUT Tom and Jutta from Gordon Hugenberger, then the senior minister of Park Street Church. My husband and I were enjoying dinner with Gordon and his wife Jane. As we discussed my writing projects, Gordon told us that there was a couple in the church who had an amazing story that needed to be written down. He explained that the husband was a Hungarian Jew and his wife had been brought up under the Nazi influence.

I was hesitant to get involved. When I was a teenager, I was traumatized by a film taken in a concentration camp by the liberating Allied soldiers. I have since learned more about the atrocities of the times. The last thing I wanted was to spend hours and possibly years staring at those realities in order to tell their story without flinching.

My husband, however, ran with this idea. It was easy to find Tom and Jutta at church, and we invited them to lunch. At an Irish pub, we were enraptured by Tom's story and his storytelling. On another Sunday, we met again to hear Jutta's story. In the next months, Tom loaned me books that told the history of Hungary during the war, a biography of Raoul Wallenberg, and another that told the story of the Hungarian Revolution. I was grateful that Tom was sensitive to the effect of descriptions of tortures and executions and had torn out the offending pages.

A couple of years after our first lunch, I got up the courage to tell Tom that if he ever wanted to get his story written down, I would love to work with him. He happily informed me that he was working with his daughter, Esther, and had 200 pages already written. I took that as a "no" and put the idea on the shelf.

In March of 2014, I received a phone call from Esther. She explained that she and her dad had been working on writing his and her mom's stories but that she had come to a place where she wanted a "real" writer to take it to the next level. Gordon Hugenberger had given her the names of a few writers in the church that he could recommend. We arranged to meet. Instead of a formal interview, we talked easily for two and a half hours and came away realizing that we each had found a new friend. Esther consulted with her parents, and we all sought the Lord's guidance. We felt that He confirmed that I was the one to work with them.

Using Tom's manuscript as my guide, I began to look for questions about details and gaps in the storyline. Then Esther and I set out to interview Tom and Jutta to fill in the missing pieces. The additions began to flesh out stories that had previously only been sketched.

As we came to the end of the interviews, I began to focus on Tom's story alone. I chose to omit explanations of the history of the times as other sources could explain the background. I also left out stories in which Tom was not personally involved. I decided to end this "public" account with their wedding and honeymoon and leave the stories of his adventures with his business, travels with the family, and life at home for the family record.

The extensive interviews gave me the opportunity to hear their voices, not only physically, but also emotionally and spiritually. I had a choice whether to change Tom's literary style or leave it as if he were speaking in front of an audience. I chose the latter. With Jutta's story as well, I have written hers as she tells it. This means that, although fluent in English, their thought processes were still influenced by their birth languages – Hungarian and German. This is at times evident in phrases and sentence structures that are unusual in English.

In February of 2016, I presented Tom with a spiral-bound copy of his story. He was elated. He read it through in the next weeks and was pleased with the result.

With the relief of his approval, I turned to Jutta's story. Again, using Tom's manuscript as my outline and adding details gleaned from the interviews, I began to piece together a consistent narrative.

I finished writing Jutta's story in November of 2017. She read it through, gave me some notes, and approved of the result. I spent the next two months working out the blending of her story with Tom's.

As their stories converged, I discovered that their memories did not always agree regarding where and when something occurred, or details about an important day, for example, how many people attended their wedding. Instead of insisting on precision or deciding whose version I should believe, I chose to let each of them tell the story as they remembered it.

In January of 2018, at the Top of the Hub, a restaurant on the fifty-second floor of the Prudential Center, overlooking the lights of Boston, I presented Jutta with a spiral-bound volume of their combined story. Her approval, along with corrections from my team of readers and editors, has finalized the copy that you now hold in your hands.

Barbara Pless
March 2018

Pronunciation and Translations

Pronunciation

Jutta – *J* is pronounced as *Y*, and the *u* rhymes with the *oo* in *book.* – Y-oo-tah.
Mutti –The *u* rhymes with the *oo* in book. M-oo-tee.
Vati – Fah-tee

Translations

German

Mutti – Mother
Vati – Father
Tante – Aunt
Onkel – Uncle
Omi, the intimate form of Oma – Grandma
Schloss – castle, manor house, stately home (In Jutta's story, the best translation would be *manor house*)
Frau – Mrs.
Fraülein – Miss
Herr – Mr.
Herrenzimmer – Private living room for men

Hungarian

Néni – aunt
Bácsi – uncle
Nagypapa – Grandpa

In the Love of the Lord

Tom and Jutta

Shalom
Jutta and for Tom.

1
Tom
Summer 1947
Budapest, Hungary

Climbing the Wrong Rock

I WAS CLINGING to the flat side of the cliff. Only the friction between my chest and the rock kept me from sliding down to sure death. My predicament was the result of one of my many foolish attempts to test and demonstrate what I could tackle.

Our Boy Scout patrol leader was sick that day and, as second in command, I had taken the opportunity to talk the boys into climbing up this rock near the top of the small mountain. The boys had suggested that I go first. They would follow when I had proven it was safe.

The rock was steep and high, but from the bottom, it appeared conquerable without serious difficulty. Formations shaped like steps would provide an easy ascent and the small but sturdy-looking bushes alongside promised handholds to help pull oneself upward. These turned out to be cheating illusions. I discovered that the steps were made of dirt blown there by the wind, and the bushes had roots which spread out on the surface and came loose at the gentlest tug.

Almost at the top, I realized that there was no way up and no way back. My feet were partly in the air.

A small crowd gathered with my troop at the bottom of the hill. A group of young tourists joined them, and once they found out the object of their curiosity, they wasted little time walking to the top of the rock along the easy trail on the other side. They formed a human chain in hopes of grabbing my hand and hauling me up to safety, but their reach was too short.

"How about pulling yourself up just a little more?" yelled the one closest to me. "I cannot, friend," I said. "It's too smooth. I have no foothold. I don't want to risk it."

"Give it a try. If you can't, we'll get another fellow in the chain," he said.

I reached up with my arms, pulled my right knee up, inched my body upward. After moving a few inches, I slipped. In a split second, I resigned myself to the fact that my life was over, and I was soon to be in the presence of my Creator.

But after sliding about a foot, *I still don't know how,* I stopped. The fellow above looked at me in shock.

"Stay where you are. Don't move an inch. We will get to you in a few minutes!" he said.

My heart was pounding as I waited. While I did not panic when I thought it was all over, I was not looking forward to more excitement and suspense.

A new man arrived and, clinging to the others in the chain, started downwards. Just as he got past three of them, he stumbled on a rock. With my chin on the cliff and my eyes looking upward, I watched as the three-pound rock rolled straight toward my head. The end looked near again. It could have knocked me off or knocked me unconscious, but it hit a small bump on the cliff about a foot above my head and bounced over me and down into the depths below. The man above me moved more carefully as he reached for my hand. Finally, I felt a strong pull upwards.

Ever since that day, I have disliked heights, and you could not chase me up a treacherous cliff even with a rifle to my head.

As I look back, I remember how I experienced the hand of God so vividly, and felt the peace that He gave when it seemed to be over. It gives me a picture of other ego-adventures in life when a challenge is attractive and everything points to success. Yet, when nearing the top, the steps turn out to be sand and the bushes come loose at the touch. Then you hang in mid-air, hopeless, until God's hand, in his loving care, pulls you up and gives you another chance – a chance to select a more appropriate goal.

2

Tom

1932-1940

Budapest

Sunny Years

I WAS BORN into a happy, middle class home. We lived in Budapest, one of the most beautifully situated cities in the world with the lovely hills, trails, and meadows of Buda on the right bank of the Danube and the bustling, well-planned, flat city of Pest on the left bank.

In the middle of the Danube, St. Margaret Island provided a giant park and playground for both children and adults with its rose gardens, well-kept trails, rock gardens, swimming pools, and a few hotels and restaurants. Outdoor concerts and theater made for pleasant evenings in the midst of the busy metropolis of two million inhabitants.

We loved Budapest, and we loved Hungary.

My parents were strong patriots. We honored Hungary's 1,000-year history and loved both the land and our people. Every national holiday was celebrated with respect and excitement. We had a hard time understanding the few who, due to concerns about the rising power of Adolf Hitler, packed up their belongings and moved to another country.

We lived near the center of the city in Pest, in a comfortable fifth-floor apartment, high enough to shield us from the noise of the traffic below. There was nothing special about our apartment – cozy, good quality, but nothing fancy – old-fashioned furniture, a big desk, a cupboard with books behind glass, a big sofa. A little balcony off the living room was our handy "outdoors," and we used it as often as we could.

The balcony afforded one of my many pranks. On nice days, I would tie a button onto a long string, long enough to reach down the five stories of our building. I would bounce the button around ladies' heads as they walked along the sidewalk. I aimed for their noses. They swatted it away, but, interestingly, only a few looked up to find out from where the button came.

I witnessed beautiful harmony between my parents who seemed to live in a permanent state of trying to cause each other joy. I can honestly say that I never, ever heard even one unloving word between them. I have no proof that they never disagreed, but if they did, their deeply rooted love must have formed the bridge to help resolve their differences.

My father was a textile manufacturer and his company's director of sales and traveled all over Europe. Before he got married, he had a girlfriend in every town. In the week preceding his marriage, he fed a suitcase's worth of love letters into the wood stove at my grandparents' place. They were from ladies he had attracted on his travels. Years after the war, his friends told me that he was one person they could never get interested in off-color stories or questionable adventures. Every woman thought my mother was the luckiest lady to catch a man like that.

This was the man my mother enjoyed surrounding with warmth and enthusiastic support. She was a happy, secure, fun-loving, and cultured woman. She had no reason or desire to challenge my father's leadership. He in turn treasured her and led her with gentleness.

The marriage relationship they demonstrated gave me unfailing optimism concerning the possibility of a truly happy, harmonious partnership and of unshakable faithfulness between husband and wife.

I could not have dreamed of better parents. We had a very warm, open relationship. Even at dinner, my parents spent quite a bit of time talking about things I could understand and welcomed my participation.

They took me to soccer games, theater, and concerts. Almost every weekend, we went on a hike, often to the mountains in the Buda part of our city that were accessible by public transportation.

Nannies

We had a maid and a few nannies in those years. One of the nannies was from Germany, and, though she did not live with us, the fifteen to twenty hours a week I spent with her became spontaneous German lessons. She did not teach me grammar, but our conversation was in German, and what I learned has stayed with me.

I loved to drag my nannies to the train station near our home. I was happy to spend hours watching the trains move in and out.

Father

My father was full of warmth and humor, and there was never a dull moment in his presence. He was my best friend, the man I loved and trusted thoroughly. I was thrilled every time anyone would say that I looked exactly like my father. There was no greater compliment for which I could ask.

Some of my favorite times were the hours my father spent with me in the city. We would walk, look at toys in a toy shop, go to the park. Usually he flavored it with a short stop for an ice cream or a raspberry drink.

As in all European countries, soccer was the most popular sport. It was the first thing a boy played once he learned to walk. No outing was imaginable without taking along a soccer ball or at least a tennis ball to kick around. My father and I even practiced at home in my mother's absence, watching carefully to not leave any trace of damage betraying our misbehavior.

My father and I built things with blocks. We played board games, and he taught me chess. We played for hours with a beautiful train set he acquired, supposedly for me. I could not help but wonder about the true motive of my most beloved father when on birthdays he presented "me" with another shiny locomotive.

My suspicion came from the occasions when my parents' close circle of friends, three couples, gathered in our home. The women sat down to chat or play rummy while the men followed my father to shelves filled with the sizable collection of "my" train set. It was playtime for the lawyer, pharmacist, bakery owner, and textile manufacturer. The floor became the site of bustling activity as trains rushed around, and the four men in their early forties did their best to maneuver the switches to avoid collisions.

My job was to operate the gates when the trains approached or departed, a job of no glamour and no challenge since the traffic across the tracks was regulated by my father and his friends. Consequently, when collisions happened, I, the "owner," just watched the men as they blamed each other, revealing the fervor and temperament of kids.

I loved playing with it with my friends, and it was a special event for them as well. When my friends were there, I was allowed to set up the twenty-five to thirty cars into two or three trains and use all of the switches, gates, and lights.

My favorite was an engine that could be driven from either end. It was a fancy high-speed car that had a dining area and comfortable compartments for its wealthy passengers. After arrival, the conductor only needed to walk through the car to start it going in the opposite direction. It was modeled on one that traveled from Budapest to Vienna at 100 kilometers per hour, a very high speed in those days.

I loved the train set, but one year I asked my father, "For my next birthday, could you buy something for ME?"

Vacations

In the summer, my father usually took four weeks of vacation. He had a remarkable ability to disconnect from his business. We often spent those precious family times on Lake Balaton, the largest lake in central Europe, or in the Bükk Mountains in northern Hungary. Occasionally, we ventured to neighboring countries. We had great times in Millstadt, Austria, and beautiful Bled, Slovenia.

One of the mornings before breakfast at Hotel Toplice in the town of Bled, Father and I went fishing from the rail of the restaurant. I happened to lean a bit too far forward and fell head first into the lake. He knew I could swim and before he helped me, he grabbed his camera to record the event. Only then did he lower the handle of his fishing rod to pull me out.

Another of the vacations was at the Hotel Royal on Lake Balaton. The dining room was in a separate building from the hotel. It had a flat roof and seated about 150 people. Light and fresh air came through six round, screenless windows near the roof on three sides of the building.

I finished lunch and asked my parents if I could leave the table. While I was loved by my parents, my presence was not sorely missed, particularly during a period of rest. The permission to leave the table was instantly and unanimously granted. It provided, or should have provided, a relaxed coffee time for my parents.

I went outside and picked up my beach ball. I was about six years old, the right age to start preparing to qualify for the national soccer team. Learning to handle the ball by using your head is an important facet of the game. I threw the ball at the side of the dining hall and bounced it back with my head. Eventually, I could do this three or four times without the ball ever touching the ground. But a moment came when the ball did not bounce back. It had entered the dining room through one of the round windows. All I could do was to run as fast and as far as I could.

My parents and the hundred and fifty other guests must have been surprised when the ball bounced from table to table splashing soup and gravy, breaking plates and glasses, and causing general devastation.

I was finally located by my father who found me hiding in one of the restrooms. It was to his credit that he understood that no ill will was involved, but the hotel manager suggested that when we would come the next year, perhaps there were other hotels we might wish to try. A postcard from that vacation that I found later read, "The weather is beautiful, the hotel could not be better, but Tom gets us into trouble at times."

Summer Camp

My parents wanted me to be able to stand on my own feet among other children, especially since I was an only child. Each summer, they signed me up for a week-long children's camp in the villa district of Svábhegy, a hilly area on the Buda side of the city. There were about forty children, excellent supervision, good food, and fun activities.

Peter was one of the six boys in our room, a real comic, one year younger than I. He loved to hold his blanket in front of him and bounce twice on his mattress before dropping on his buttocks and covering himself. This was his final act each night, which he did for both entertainment and to show off a bit.

I saw potential in his routine for a prank. One night while Peter brushed his teeth in the bathroom, I alerted my roommates to cooperate with me. Our mattresses were in three sections. I replaced the middle one on Peter's bed with a shallow wash basin half-filled with water and pulled the sheet over it. The plan was that two of us would challenge him to start at the very end of his bed. This would make for a longer flight after the second bounce and would ensure that he would not notice the change in his mattress.

Peter enjoyed our unanimous interest in his routine and stood up at the end of his bed. We held our breath as he bounced twice and landed on the basin, generating a splash of water and a roar of laughter across the whole room. Peter blushed like an overripe tomato and yelled, "I know who is behind this trick! Tom, you are a terrible rascal! Just wait, I'll get you later!"

All this without any investigation! This was not the last time I was exposed to injustice, the rude violation of legal process.

"Beware of Tom" was a saying.

Tenth Prank

In second grade, I committed enough pranks that my father gave me a warning: "When your mother reports to me the tenth bad incident, you will get a licking you will remember for the rest of your life." While Father radiated love and good humor, I did not doubt for a moment that he meant business.

It took me three weeks to get to nine.

One afternoon after school, my friends and I were playing on Kossuth Square near the Parliament Building. The boys agreed with me that it would be fun to hide behind the bushes and throw pebbles at the streetcars rushing by. Unfortunately, one of my pebbles hit the conductor's side window, smashing it into pieces. The streetcar stopped, the conductor jumped off and ran after us. He must have been told who the culprit was because he ignored the others. His legs were longer than mine, and the distance between us decreased rapidly. In last minute despair, I climbed up on the Kossuth monument, hoping that he could not follow me. There he was, huffing, red-faced, and angry as he tried to climb up after me. The spectators had a great time! Within minutes, a policeman who had been guarding the Parliament Building arrived. He removed me from the monument and took me straight to my school principal. The principal banned all students from talking to me for a week and issued a warning to my parents indicating I would be expelled with the next serious incident.

When Mother placed the warning in front of my father for him to sign, both Mother and I were slightly shaking. Both of us knew that nine plus one equals ten, and we were wondering if Father was going through the same calculation. He read the story, signed it, handed it to me, and asked Mother if lunch was ready.

I usually felt free to ask questions or tell stories, but my brain seemed to be paralyzed. It was the quietest lunch we ever had, and I did not like it. After lunch, as was his habit, Father sat in the comfortable armchair and opened the paper. I tried to make conversation, but nothing worked. All I got were short answers while his eyes were fixed on the paper.

Finally, I decided to come up with a question needing specific help from him. I came near – I should have made a bigger circle around him – and got ready to present the case. With one swift move the paper was dropped, and I got a backhanded slap which sent me flying toward the radiator. During the flight, I saw a few stars, felt some warmth, and a strange dizziness. As I slumped to the floor, I realized that Father had kept his word. A tear or two rolled down my face as a result of the pain, but the punishment was so clearly just and my confidence in my father's love was so firm that crying did not make sense. In fact, I felt guilty for provoking this ugly scene. It was almost a relief to have it over with.

He calmly continued to read his paper while my Mother collected my remains on her lap. He had displayed no anger before and none after the event. To him, it was a simple transaction to reconcile the balance I had willingly upset over the past months. He did not have to apologize because he knew he was right.

Of course, some may be horrified by such parental corporal discipline. As far as I am concerned, it was the best and quickest medicine to cure a defect in my developing character. I did not become good as a result, but I became less of a nuisance.

Table Tennis

I also knew some successes.

Table tennis was very popular in summer camps. This fast, exciting game required little space and kept not only the players, but also the spectators entertained. Once, I managed to become champion in our camp and got into the final of the singles inter-camp championship. My opponent was much taller than I and made me feel I had little chance of winning. I just wanted to do my best.

After three minutes of practice, the judge made us go for the serve. Goliath won the starting advantage. The start was drowned by our camp's roaring, "Go, Tom, go! Go, go, go!"

Within eighteen minutes, Goliath beat me 21 to 15. I was surprised by an even stronger, "Go, Tom, go! Go, go, go!" I started serving game two and pulled ahead to 9 to 11. Then came the onslaught, and Goliath was leading 20 to 12. Some of my friends left as they did not want to embarrass me by watching my demise. Having little to lose, I decided to show that I wouldn't crumble.

To my and everybody's amazement, I won one point after another. The cheering got stronger after every point.

My gang went wild when I caught up to him 20 to 20 and then continued the series of hits to beat him 22 to 20!

I won the third game and the match, and my gang lifted me on their shoulders. It felt awesome!

Losing the first game, choosing to give it my all no matter what, and then winning from a score of 12 to 20 became a lifetime motivation to fight, even when there seems to be no hope. But even now, I know no mercy when it comes to table tennis. I am not the nice guy who feels bad for the other person.

Shabbat

Meaningful friendships, laughter, outings, fun, culture – an eventful, peaceful life is what I remember during those years. I was guarded by the strength of a cohesive home where God was honored.

On Friday nights, my mother lit the candle and said the Shabbat prayer before we went to synagogue. While there was considerable social chatter during a good part of the service, a special awe filled me every time the rabbi raised the curtain of the Holy of Holies and solemn silence filled the sanctuary.

On greater Jewish holidays, we would gather at the home of my grandparents on my mother's side. The 100-year-old apartment near St. Stephen's Basilica had fourteen-foot ceilings and hardwood floors. The antique scent and flavor was enhanced by a cozy fire in the wood stove in the sitting room.

Once, on Rosh Hashanah, my parents told me to make sure to sleep an hour in the afternoon so that I could stay up late. I pretended. My father asked me if I slept, and I said yes. Then I started to get a bellyache and thought that God must be real because He knew that I had lied. The pain of the stomachache was unforgettably bad.

3

Tom

1940-1941

Budapest

Gathering Clouds

MY FATHER'S employees did not care that their boss was Jewish. He respected their religion as they respected his. Every year, he delivered Christmas gifts, baskets of fine vegetables, fruits, or chocolates, to the homes of his employees. They appreciated that this Jewish boss cared about their Christmas. I often went with him, and I sensed a genuine, mutual love on those visits.

On one of the Jewish holidays when we were at my grandparents' apartment, my father confessed to us that his world seemed to be starting to crumble. The government was passing laws that restricted educational opportunities for Jews as well as limiting their businesses and job prospects. He was a strong patriot, and it hurt him terribly as he realized that the country had started to disown him because he was Jewish.

My father was my most beloved, best friend. How could they do this to him? And if they treated him this way, what kind of allegiance should I have to this country? At the age of nine, I clenched my fist in anger.

The colorful, joyous life I had experienced gave way to increasing concern about our future. The gathering clouds which followed the sunny years turned into the steadily increasing rumble of thunderclaps as the storm approached.

Persecution

A new phenomenon was a sudden urge by some Jews to become Christians. This did not have anything to do with a change in convictions. It was a last resort to become "one of them," at least on paper.

Some newly converted Jewish children became quite devout Christians. Others got carried away with their new identity. One boy in my class, now a "Christian," went a little too far and called me a "dirty Jew" a few weeks after his conversion. I expressed my displeasure with his arrogance triggered by the newly acquired identity. His face was bloody when they took him to the ambulance. I got away with only a strong reprimand by my teacher who apparently felt that I had reason to be upset.

Father Called into the Army

About this time, we received a special delivery letter announcing that the Hungarian Army was calling Father to report for military service in the response to the advance of the Russian army. We did not feel that this was extraordinary as many were being called into the war effort.

Tom – 1940-1941

Father was a great letter writer. I remember the excitement every time a letter from him came from the front lines. It always contained a few lines written especially to me, his big ten-year-old son who was supposed to take care of Mother. We in turn sent letters and parcels with goodies, warm socks, flannel pajamas, sausages, cheese – things that wouldn't spoil because it would take several days before he got them. We also sent enough for him to share with a man in his squadron who did not have a family to care for him.

Occasionally, he would tell us about his life, but nothing that would cause him trouble. We knew that his letters would be censored by the army. He did tell us that the stars on the collar of his uniform had been removed and that he and the other Jews had to wear a yellow armband instead.

An occasion to see each other occurred when my father's squadron returned briefly to Vác, Hungary, and we were allowed to visit him one Sunday afternoon.

The commander allowed the group to put on a variety show for the visitors, using the many different talents incorporated in this group of creative but doomed humanity. I can still hear the Santa Lucia solo accompanied by a guitar as it rolled over the meadow and the laughter during the skits which brought to us bits of their daily lives.

The highlight for my parents must have been the three-hour free time when they were allowed to leave the camp and be together in privacy. I was left behind with a kindly bachelor, a former circus strongman, who seemed to have a knack for dealing with children. We had a great time listening to his fascinating stories. He was a gentle, lonesome man. This was the friend my father had taken under his wing and for whom we were instructed to always send two pieces of the same thing as we packed the parcels.

We heard later that my father's generosity got him into trouble with the commanders. He saved some of his food to share with Russian and Polish Jews who were being held behind fences in a separate camp. For this kindness, he was transferred to a special punishment squad. This put him in the front line to dig ditches in enemy fire, an efficient arrangement because if the bullets missed, the ditches grew deeper, and if they did not, there were fewer Jews with which to bother.

After two years, my father's letters stopped coming. Then an official note came informing us of his disappearance: "No information is available on his whereabouts." We chose to believe that he had become a prisoner of war and, because of the rumors about the treatment of Jews in the army, we decided that he was probably safer in the hands of the future victors. Also, if he returned to Hungary, he could end up in one of the Nazi death camps. We did not lose hope of reuniting with him after the war would be over.

4
Tom
Spring 1944
Budapest

Nazi Invasion

ON MARCH 19, 1944, my mother and I woke up to the sounds of marching feet and the rumbles of heavy vehicles. The main street was a block and a half from our building and was on the route of the German army coming into our city. When we turned on the radio, we heard German military marches and the announcement, "At 6:00 a.m. this morning, upon the request of our Head of State Admiral Horthy, the forces of our mighty German ally entered our borders to provide protective occupation against the approaching Russian forces."

I felt the weight of the situation as much as a twelve year old could, but fortunately, I did not realize the connection between the German presence and the occasionally mentioned camps, the details of which had been kept from me. The noisy events of the day brought me neither joy nor worry, but admittedly some excitement and fascination burst into my life. Something important was happening, and I was right on the scene.

Almost overnight, the Germans were visible everywhere. Impeccably dressed officers took full advantage of the situation, parading the streets with an arrogant air of superiority and power. I remember one officer walking on the main street. He was a tall man with shiny boots and carried a riding crop. He looked like he was saying, "I am the boss here now. Look at me."

The Hungarian Arrow Cross party, established ten years earlier along the same principles and with the same agenda as the Nazis, were now free to come out in the open. Their actions against us Jews were as bad as or even worse than the Nazis.

The first air raid warning caught us by surprise. Before the sirens began to howl, Russian bombs could be heard, and blinding flares changed deep night darkness into an eerie light. All of us headed for the cellar that had become the air raid shelter for our five-story building. The elevators held only two to four people, so thirty or forty of us were spiraling down the stairs in pajamas and nightgowns covered by overcoats.

The raids lasted from fifteen minutes to half an hour and occurred about once a week. Eventually, they increased to two or three times a week, and later, two or three times a day, lasting from a few minutes to several hours. The frequent gathering in the cellar turned isolated neighbors into a community. We brought compact kits of food and other necessities which made us more flexible about leaving everything behind. It even became a fun thing because I could meet the other children in my building. I always brought my chess set and my toys and had fun playing with them.

We had a portable radio, which told us where the bombings were happening. Someone purchased a map with little holes and different colored sticks for the different types of warnings. When we heard the locations announced on the radio, we would mark them with the sticks and then watch which way the air raids were moving.

At first, we were not too worried about being bombed because the five stories above us would be a good protection, but as the sound of the bombs hit closer and closer, we could not help being a bit scared. On the other hand, we knew that more air raids meant that the Russians were coming closer. The closer they came, the sooner would come the end of the war. We were so grateful for the courage of the Allied airmen, risking their lives under enemy fire to liberate us. I prayed for their safety as the bombs they dropped exploded around us.

Yellow Star

A few days after the first air raid, an announcement appeared on posters everywhere declaring a new law which forced Jews to place a yellow, three-inch Star of David on the left breast of whatever clothing they would wear in public. We had to make it ourselves according to their dimensions. Initially, I wore this star with pride, but I soon found out that it invited scorn and abuse. I did not dare to not wear it, however, because of the greater punishments that were declared.

Some of my former buddies at school stopped greeting me. Others sneered at the star. Many of our neighbors no longer returned our hello. The owner of the grocery store put out a sign stating, "We don't serve Jews," and the woman who had been my mother's hairdresser for decades refused to serve her. There were a few shopkeepers who still did business with us, and we had a few friendly neighbors including the wife of the janitor of our building.

Hate posters appeared throughout the city depicting Jews as "Christ Killers." A suffering, crucified Christ was shown being stabbed in the chest by a fat businessman with a hooked nose wearing a yellow star on his jacket, grinning from ear to ear. Beneath the knife, blood dripped from His wound onto the rosy cheeks of a precious little Hungarian girl in national costume. The caption read: "THEY KILLED HIM!"

I had been taught by my parents to respect Christianity, the religion professed by my dear Bandi Bácsi who married into our family. We viewed the charming Bethlehem scenes, angels, shepherds, and lambs as expressions of religious tales centered around the baby Jesus and his mother Mary. I did not associate Mary with the Madonna, the worshipped patron saint of Hungary. I actually thought the Madonna was a deified Roman Catholic nun from Italy, so well was her Jewish identity masked in her public representation. Neither did I realize Jesus was a Jew. Nor did I have a problem with the crucified Jesus who I thought suffered because he pretended to have divine claims. However, this poster indicated to me that Jesus had to be the most likely cause of our persecution because of the accusation that we Jews had caused his horrible death. Finally, I had an explanation for all that hatred towards us, which I had thought was rooted mainly in our being descendants of a different race. This was a revelation which resulted in a violent turn in my soul against Christ and Christianity.

In school, those of us of the Jewish race were separated from the Gentiles for religion classes. In the classes for the Gentiles, split between Catholics and Protestants, the guilt of Jews in the murder of Christ was an oft-discussed topic. They were taught that a person's Jewish ancestry justified his being persecuted and abused. After those classes let out, we were mocked for what they called an odd and obsolete faith, and they subjected us to malicious treatment and hostile taunts.

One teacher stood up for us. He taught Latin and was the head teacher responsible for our class. He was a devout Catholic, but it seemed like he had asked to be responsible for my Jewish class in order to have the authority to protect us. He was a man of extraordinary charm coupled with uncompromising but loving discipline of his students. We felt safe under his supervision. He was a veteran of the First World War and was too highly respected to get into trouble.

5

Tom

Summer 1944

Budapest

Jewish House

IN JUNE OF 1944, there was a decree that Jews had to move into houses designated by a yellow star above the door. Fortunately, ours was one of these, so we did not have to move. My aunt, my grandfather, and my mother's aunt and uncle all moved in with us within a week. Since there was little extra room in our apartment, where six of us shared three rooms, they had to leave most of their furniture and belongings behind.

I loved having family members join us. With Béla Bácsi we had a strong man protecting us again. He was in his sixties, but he was a ball of energy, a master of many skills, and had a great sense of humor. He was a prankster extraordinaire, and an inexhaustible source of tricks and jokes. He taught me to fix anything, whether we had the right tools and materials or not. He was also skilled at packing and, when we were still in contact with my father, had helped Mother send maximum content within the size limit permitted by the military.

His wife, Rózus Néni, was the darling of our family and my mother's mentor after her mother was deceased. She was wise, gentle, and beautiful, and being a skilled diplomat, was the right partner for the occasionally volatile Béla Bácsi.

Bözsike Néni was the oldest of my mother's siblings, the angel of the family. If she found out anyone had a need, she took care of it. Once when I was hungry and it was not lunchtime, she brought me a slice of toast. She would notice if I needed a pencil, and she would find one for me.

She took over my grandfather's dressmaking business and counted Mrs. Varga, the wife of the Minister of Industry, among her famous clients.

Grűnbaum Nagypapa was eighty at this time, a proud, disciplined man without an extra ounce on his body. He had kept in shape through careful eating habits and long walks, which he interrupted with a half-hour rest at Elizabeth Square where he fed the doves and chatted with older folk he had gotten to know over the years. Having been removed from his neighborhood, the move hit him hardest. He became somewhat bitter and spent much of his time sitting in a comfortable armchair smoking his pipe and listening to the radio. He was no friend of elevators, and having impaired vision and hearing, he seldom ventured out except to our small balcony.

Radio

At night, most of us huddled around the radio, listening to shortwave broadcasts from the BBC and other Allied stations. In addition to being the only source of reliable information, just hearing "The Star-Spangled Banner," "Yankee Doodle," or the British national anthem boosted our morale.

Soon we received another directive that made listening to Allied broadcasts a crime of treason. To safeguard against a charge of disobeying this restriction, many Jews, including our family, took their radios to a local shop where they blocked the tuner from moving to the non-local stations. Suddenly, all contact with the free world was cut off, and all hopes and dreams for the future became vague. Now, it took all of our inner resources to cope with each new day.

Curfew

Soon a further restriction limited us Jews to leaving our homes only during the hours from 9:00 to 11:00 a.m. and from 3:00 to 5:00 p.m.

Every day, as soon as the curfew was lifted, we found a reason to leave the house and get some fresh air. Within minutes, we would be at the neighborhood playground forming soccer teams where we were able to let out our compressed energy on the battered tennis balls that we used for the games. There were many games where we had to run for our lives to be home before the curfew resumed.

I loved classical music almost more than soccer. I underlined the detailed radio program for the week and would run back to the apartment to listen to the music before returning to the game. Adhering to the music schedule was a way I could have a sense of control over my life.

The daily deprivation of time in the streets and parks forced us to use our balcony and the tiny courtyard inside the walls of the building to get fresh air. The courtyard was intended primarily as a space for cleaning rugs, which were hung on a horizontal rod and beaten with tough straw "prakkers" to remove the dust. Now it was a frequent sight to see thirty or forty Jews sitting, chatting, and pacing in the 30-by-30-foot yard for hours at a time.

We children were no longer allowed to attend school. On one hand, we enjoyed our unlimited freedom, but we realized that we were cut off from pursuing our education.

Cousin Fun

My best breaks in these times were the almost daily button-soccer games played on the floor with my cousin Gyuri who was two years my senior and the son of the deceased, beloved Bandi Bácsi. Because Gyuri was half Gentile, he could visit us freely after school hours.

Button soccer was played with two teams of eleven "players" made of one to three clothing buttons glued on top of each other. Pressing one's thumb and index finger tightly together on the edge of the top of a player would make the player slide out and hit the smaller button "ball," pushing it forward. We filed an angled flat area on one side of each of the players, giving them the ability to lift the "ball" over obstacles and allowing it to eventually land in the adversary's goal. We loved this game and with fervor pursued victory for hours at a time. It was a terrific distraction from the darkening reality of our situation.

Fifteen-year-old Gyuri did not make these visits without risk. Gentiles were expected to sever their relationships with Jews. One afternoon, when bringing cookies baked for us by his mother, an Arrow Cross man noticed him entering our house. Waiting for him to exit, the man grabbed Gyuri and beat him up, leaving his face and body badly bruised. Gyuri still visited, but with more fear than before.

Mary's Class

Late in the summer of 1944, it was rumored that conversion to Christianity would allow us to wear a white star instead of the yellow one, be kept in a "white ghetto," and escape deportation to the death camps. Mother approached me with the idea of taking part in a course to be given by a Jewish lady who had become a Christian while visiting England before the war.

"I just want to find out enough about the fundamentals of Christianity to be sure I don't desecrate our Jewish tradition if I pretend conversion," Mother said. "Do you mind if Mary Hajós would come to our apartment a few times and educate us on this subject? I would not forgive myself if we were deported just because I did not perform the formality of conversion to Christianity."

I replied, "I would rather have my right arm dry up than walk into a Christian church. If you want to convert, that's your business, but I don't want to take part."

Mary Hajós was an accomplished teacher of the English language and of graphology. Her husband Emil, who spoke seven languages, was an assistant to the Secretary of State prior to the war. Both were devoted Jewish Christians.

When my mother introduced me to Mary, I tried hard to be reasonably polite. She radiated kindness and invited me to attend the meetings. This was a tactical error on her part as it made me suspect that the whole project was a plot to lay a trap for me. I flatly refused and excused myself.

Instead, I teamed up with Béla Bácsi to perform work projects in the adjacent room that involved hammering or banging pots and pans. She must have had a hard time overcoming the background noise, but Mary was not about to give up. Neither was she willing to get revenge or even show resentment. The meaner I got, the kinder she became, which frustrated me to no end, but I was puzzled about her source of strength.

As far as I was concerned, I felt no animosity toward any relative or acquaintance who professed a Christian belief. Based on my recent experiences, however, I rejected what I perceived to be Christianity with its churches and clergy.

When the course was over, some, including my mother, got "converted," at least on paper. Mary obtained the appropriate documents, and the ceremony of baptism – sprinkling with water – was performed.

6
Tom
Fall 1944
Budapest

Mother Taken

ONE MORNING, we heard the ringing of the gong belonging to the janitor of our building. When we assembled at his door, an Arrow Cross patrol leader announced that Jews between the ages of fifteen and sixty-five had fifteen minutes to be ready for a long march.

This meant that I, age twelve, and my eighty-year-old grandfather could stay, but my mother, aunt, great uncle, and great aunt had to go. The parting was a heartbreak. We didn't know if we would ever see each other again, but we had no time to cry. Frankly, due to the constant threats to our safety, I simply felt numb. Mother handed me some money, and they started down the flights of stairs.

The sight from our window as I watched this group of forty or fifty, including my mother, being marched away by armed Arrow Cross guards was heart-rending.

I shared with Grandpa that they expected the few leftovers – children and oldsters – to be transferred into a section of Budapest which was set up as a walled-in ghetto.

I did not realize the eighty-year-old tailor was not prepared for another move. He stuffed his beloved pipe and retired to his room and, as I discovered later, consumed his carefully hidden bottle of sleeping pills for a long, undisturbed rest.

It was a bleak situation – stuck in an apartment with an octogenarian and a few dozen fish swimming around in a large aquarium. I had no idea what was going to happen next, which was a way of life to which we had gotten accustomed; but facing it alone was a new experience.

The cloudy day provided a matching background to my thoughts as I stared through the window at the distant mountains of Buda. I gave my fish a late lunch and completely forgot about my grandfather who, I thought, must be having an extended nap after the distress of seeing his family leaving him. Dusk was setting in when I was ready to continue my life and pick up my undefined responsibilities.

I walked over to Grandpa's small room and knocked at the door. There was no answer and no sign of light through the gap under the door. Grandpa was hard of hearing, so I knocked harder. I opened the door and saw him still sound asleep four hours after he had said a sobbing goodbye to his loved ones. Leaning closer, I noticed that his eyes were open and his hand was holding a sleeping pill bottle that had no pills inside. He wasn't breathing.

I rushed downstairs and told Mrs. Döblin, the janitor's wife, that it looked like Grandpa had committed suicide. She came up with me and, with tears in her eyes, promised me she would call the ambulance to take Grandpa to the first aid station in order to take care of appropriate procedures.

They came and, after touching his cold hand, lifted him up and carried his frail body away. I did not think to ask where they were taking him. We never found out where he was buried or cremated.

It was strange to be all alone in the apartment. I made toast and a cup of tea, took a shower, and went to bed. I did not try to think about anything, letting thoughts about tomorrow rest for the night.

Close Call

I woke up the next morning after a deep sleep, still feeling numb, hoping that Mother and the other family members were all right. In my mind, this fifth-floor apartment had changed overnight from my home into simply a furnished shelter. I resigned myself to becoming a temporary hermit in it.

The food in the kitchen was sufficient for several days. I made scrambled eggs mixed with a variety of vegetables and bacon, drank some milk, and fed the fish. It took me a while to find something with which to kill time as I waited for a next event to put me onto a track leading somewhere. I was on hold.

I decided to clean the seventy-gallon aquarium. Once I had a project, I started to feel like a person again. It was a two to three-hour job into which I could anchor my attention, and gave me the excuse to postpone any planning or decisions.

Just as I opened the window to let in some fresh air, the janitor's gong sounded. Those of us who were "leftover" tenants gathered around the janitor. He informed us that the Arrow Cross wanted all of us, without regard to age or condition, to line up in fifteen minutes prepared for a long walk.

Most of us already had our hiking boots and socks ready and our knapsacks packed with essential items. We knew how little time we would be allowed to leave our home behind. I hurried upstairs, grabbed the knapsack, put fresh water in the bottle, poured a lot of fish food into the aquarium, and looked around one last time. I stepped out the door, only to stare into the shocked, but resolute, faces of Mrs. Alföldy and her sister, our wonderful Gentile next-door neighbors.

"We will not let them take you away, Tom," they said as they grabbed my arm. "Come in and hide under the bed in our bedroom."

"Are you aware of what you are doing?" I responded. "You are defying the Arrow Cross. If they find me in your apartment, they will kill you even before they tackle me."

"Leave that between God and us. Move fast!"

The chance to avoid being taken away blinded my conscience, and I dashed under their master bed. Then I tried to figure out how I would respond to an Arrow Cross henchman peering at me as he searched the place for hiding Jews. I shuddered at the thought of such an encounter. He could blow my head off on the spot and just leave me there.

Suddenly, I had a better idea. How about hiding in the toilet chamber and pretend I had violent diarrhea? With the Alföldy sisters' approval, I went to the toilet and assumed the most natural position on the seat. After about ten minutes, the doorbell rang and an Arrow Cross man entered the Alföldy home.

My heart was pounding. I shot up a quick, desperate prayer as I heard heavy steps pass. The Alföldy sisters saw him thrust his gun with a long bayonet under every bed, armchair, and sofa. On his way out, he opened the first two of three identical storage room doors to my left and, figuring that my door was that of a third storage area, he did not bother opening it.

When they left, we were in a daze. The three of us embraced in utter amazement.

"It is our joy to care for you in the absence of your dear parents," Mrs. Alföldy said. "Let us know if we can be of any help while you stay in the house. You had better stay inside your apartment. Who knows if someone will report having seen you? Should you need anything, we can always get it for you."

With this wise, comforting advice, I returned to my apartment next door. I dropped my knapsack and had a sandwich to calm my nerves. I sat down and reflected on how I had just experienced love and heroism displayed so vividly by real heroes.

I now feel like the protection of God and His angels must have been at work in the hearts and home of these two courageous ladies. Some may question the idea that God protected me, when so many others in similar situations perished. Only He knows the reasons for what to us appears as God intervening differently in different situations.

I had no idea where to go from there, but I knew that I had better find some other shelter before I got caught either by the next group of Arrow Cross or by the Hungarian Nazis who would be chosen to occupy our home.

As I stood up and walked to the window, the setting sun gave the late fall dusk a soft golden hue. Where? To whom? How? When? These thoughts were flaring up when I heard a gentle knock at the door. I walked to the door, wondering if the Arrow Cross had discovered that I had stayed behind. To my astonishment, the daughter of the nearby shoemaker was standing there. Her father's store had been one of the few in the neighborhood where friendliness toward us Jews had remained unchanged. The young girl was the bearer of good news.

Mother's Story

"Your mother is waiting in our store. I was sent to make sure the house was free of raiders and to see if any of your family still remained."

I assured her that it seemed safe for my mother to enter the house. She left and this time I could hardly wait for the next knock on the door. It took only a few minutes before it came.

"Don't worry, it is me."

I tore open the door, and there was Mother. We embraced each other while we sobbed and laughed. It was a dream beyond any hope!

Mother explained to me what had happened.

After the Arrow Cross led Mother, my aunts and uncle, and the others out of our apartment building, they stopped at a street corner a block away where they were separated by age. The elderly were led to a newly established ghetto near the main synagogue. These included my aunts and uncle. Mother and the other younger people were forced to march across the Margaret Bridge to a brick factory in the older section of Buda. After they arrived, they were given a short rest before they would be lined up to march to an "Austrian military factory."

As the crowd waited for orders to march, Mother noticed a large pile of bricks. Although aware that the risk of being discovered would mean immediate death, she decided to hide behind the pile. She held her breath and hoped to stay unnoticed while, as dusk fell, over 300 Jews were led away. Ripping off her yellow star, she peeked around the pile of bricks to see if any personnel had remained behind. When it looked safe, she slipped into a corner behind an even larger pile of bricks. Figuring it safer to stay overnight than to risk the dangers of being seen on the street after curfew, she found some hay and rags, covered herself, and managed to catch some sleep.

In the morning, she awoke to the arrival of another group of Jews with more Arrow Cross guards. She prayed incessantly to not be discovered as she watched yet three more groups pass through during the day. By late afternoon, the last group had left on their march. This time she decided to escape.

Even though the Nazis had developed a sixth sense for spotting frightened-looking, shabbily dressed Jews out on the street after curfew, Mother made it safely to the cobbler's store without being stopped.

It now seems to me that at the same time that I was under protection in the apartment, she too was under God's protection during this dangerous journey.

"I am glad you are not marching toward Germany! You probably thought I had been taken somewhere as well with the possibility of never finding each other. True?" I asked her.

"Absolutely! I was overcome with fear an hour ago when the cobbler's wife told me about the raid on the building this afternoon. How did you manage to avoid being taken away?"

I shared with her the story, after which she asked about her father, my Grandpa. She sobbed when she learned the way he had departed and realized she had no chance either to alter the past or to find his body and fulfill the last obligations as required by Jewish law.

Mother set her hands to preparing a sandwich supper. I learned she had not had anything to eat in thirty hours. After the meal, we had only one thought: to find safer refuge. Not wanting to take the risk of escaping after curfew, we decided to stay overnight. Mother said she had a promising solution in mind, but the day had been long for both of us, and we left planning the details for the next day.

We began to decide on the essentials we would pack into two handbags. We were so overwhelmed by our unexpected reunion that we did not waste time worrying about leaving behind even the things dear to us. Anything left behind would go to the new tenants who would be rewarded for their loyalty to the Arrow Cross with the right to take possession of our home and everything it contained.

Mother embraced me as she stood in the center of our living room with a tear rolling down her cheek.

"Tom, think about the wonderful years we were privileged to have here with your dear father, our family, and friends. Let's cherish the memories we can take with us and not let our losses cast a shadow over these treasures that nobody can tear away from us. I thank God for your being a real support for me in an unknown future."

After a hug and a kiss, we said goodnight and retired for a somewhat uneasy rest. "Who knows when the next knock on the door comes?" we wondered as we fell asleep.

7
Tom
Fall 1944
Budapest

Move to the Swiss House

WHEN WE woke up the next morning, the reality of abandoning our beloved apartment truly sank in. It was not the things, it was the memory-filled home we felt sorry to leave behind.

During our breakfast of half-dried rolls, butter, and hot milk, Mother showed me a document she had found in our mailbox upon her return from the brick factory. It came from Mary Hajós, the Jewish Christian lady who had held classes in our home. The document was a "Certificate of Protection" from the Swiss government. It was made out in Mother's and my names and would allow us to take shelter at Szent István Park 22. This residence was one of a few dozen "protected houses" in an area of the 5th District of the Pest side of the city.

What timing! It seemed as if someone were looking out for us, giving us the direction we needed on the very day we had to make such an urgent, crucial decision. This offer allowed us to avoid the overcrowded Jewish ghetto set up near the main synagogue close to the center of the city. Despite having no assurance that we would be accepted into the house to which we were assigned, Mother and I decided to take advantage of the documents.

We said a grateful goodbye to our dear neighbors, the Alföldy sisters. They were pleased to see that I was no longer alone and wished us well.

To avoid possible contact with our Gentile neighbors, we used the elevator instead of the stairs, and despite a curfew being in place, we slipped out of the house. A sandwich and a bottle of water in my coat pocket gave me some comfort in case we were not admitted to the house and would have to go on searching for refuge.

Without exchanging a word, we watched people around us on the street. We did not want to attract the attention of Arrow Cross men on the prowl to arrest Jews out after curfew or Gentile acquaintances who might recognize us and report us to the police. It was a twenty-minute walk in fear along streets we had walked so many times in our attractive neighborhood. While this was no time for nostalgia, I could not help thinking of pleasant memories as we walked past the theater of comedies Vigszinház, restaurant Fischer, dessert coffeehouse Lukács, the movie theater Lloyd, and so many other places we enjoyed when we were considered legitimate members of Hungarian society. Now we were pariahs looking for shelter in a house of strangers.

Life in the Swiss House

When we arrived at Szent István Park 22, we were relieved to see the Swiss colors on the plate above the door. We rang the janitor's doorbell hoping for the best. He looked at us with suspicion. There must have been many attempts by Jews seeking refuge without Swiss protection certificates. He looked at ours, motioned us to follow, and knocked at the door of Apartment 1.

When the door opened, we could see a lot of people inside. Some were chatting, others were reading, children were playing. The women who were preparing food turned toward us with a look of concern as room had to be made for two more in a two-room apartment which already housed over twenty people. The janitor asked for the man who was in charge. He handed him our papers and, heading toward the stairs, turned back and said, "You are full now. I will not direct more people to you."

As fortunate as we were to have been the last two people for which this apartment still had room, at the time we were numb, and did not give it much thought.

"Put down your bags and find a place for yourselves," the man in charge said before he started his orientation session with us. "We are all in the same boat. You had better give up any ideas about comfort or silence. It is better than having to join eighty people in a cattle car rolling to Germany. You still have an hour before curfew is over to go out and get some food. You can prepare it in the kitchen once others are done with theirs. We love onions, but we've agreed to abstain from stuff generating a strong smell. We get along well here. We're hoping the Russians will deliver us before we get into each other's hair. I hope you will help us survive without much trouble. We lie down to sleep around 10:00 p.m. We have two double beds for the oldest or the sick, which we do not have yet, thank God. Try not to get sick. Stay away from food that is not fresh enough and dress warmly when you go out. There is minimal medical help around here. Good luck!"

We sat down in a corner, opened our sandwiches, and were offered a cup of tea by someone who noticed us trying to get used to the situation.

"Do you play chess?" a boy my age asked me.

"Sure!" I responded confidently.

"Come on! I have a box we can put the set on," the fellow said. "I have been trying to find someone to play chess with since yesterday. You are the first one in this place who knows how to play. I am glad you came."

I gave him a chance to win, to assure he would want to play again since I could not figure out what else one could do in this place. Mother made quick friends of two young ladies who were trying to knit something like a glove.

We were "in."

Just before bedtime, the apartment leader announced, "Showtime!"

The lights were turned off, the shades were opened, and we gathered at the rear windows of the house, which faced east. Occasional flashes of light from cannon shots in the distance illuminated the sky, then faded from view. It was like watching a fireworks display from far away. Russian troops were discharging their deadly cargo aimed at the resisting forces protecting Budapest.

Although the sounds of the shots were distant, many felt they were a bit stronger than in the days prior. These lights – a sign that the Soviets were closer each day – reflected joy in our eyes and kept alive our hope for surviving.

After indulging in the view for a few minutes, we closed the shades and began preparations for the night, placing mattresses and blankets on the floor and taking our turns in the only bathroom.

Mother and I put down our unused clothing as bedding and covered ourselves with our winter coats. We attempted to get as good a rest as possible under the circumstances. While we had far less comfort than we were used to, being part of a group was somewhat reassuring. After two or three days, we were accustomed to the inconveniences, and we took our new environment in stride.

Light Shows

The end seemed to be approaching both audibly and visibly. The sounds of anti-aircraft guns and cannons, and military police driving by, and ambulance sirens were enveloped in the continuously increasing rumble of heavy Russian artillery. It sounded like thunder approaching very slowly but steadily. The news media denied this and reported that a major regrouping of our defense was in process in the western part of the country in preparation for a counter assault on the Russians.

By mid-December, the light shows became even more significant. We could now easily associate the sounds with the lights. With the aid of a stopwatch, we could calculate their distance from us, checking the elapsed time between a high flash and a big rumble. All day, we looked forward to these evening performances. The area where we stayed was of no military interest, so we did not feel threatened by these bombings. When we filed back into our crowded rooms, the standard question was this: "Had the activity of the flashes increased, and did they appear closer than yesterday?" Whenever the consensus was in the affirmative, we put our heads on our pillows with a little more hope.

Constant Air Raids

Beginning in December 1944, events happened in quick succession. There were so many air raids that the authorities no longer bothered turning on the sirens. Even if they had, the air raid shelter could not have held all of us, so we agreed it would be reserved for mothers with small children.

The Russians were within sixty miles, approaching fast, but too slowly for us.

Hanukkah

When Hanukkah approached, I made a menorah out of a wooden candy box. Starting on December 11, at the mature age of twelve and three-quarters, I led services in the apartment every night for eight nights with all of the thirty-odd members of my "congregation" participating. There was, of course, no other place for them to go, but everybody enjoyed a bit of festivity. I had been a good Hebrew student at school, which meant that I could read Hebrew quite fluently and with decent pronunciation. We were never taught to understand what we read, and I assumed that it must not have been too important as long as God heard it.

No Trucks

One morning in late December, we were awakened at 4:00 a.m. with the bad news:

"Line up in the backyard. Take your belongings. Trucks will soon arrive to move you to another location!"

We were given twenty minutes to get ready. We gathered in the backyard and stood across from the machine-gun-toting Arrow Cross men who paced up and down reveling in their power over us.

After about an hour and a half, word came that the trucks which were supposed to take us across the Danube to the northwestern border of the city would not be coming. The plan was to use the trucks under the cover of darkness to avoid the scene of Jews being herded across town in broad daylight. With great relief, we returned to our apartment and tried to live for another day, wondering what the next night would bring.

The next morning exactly at 4:00 a.m., we took part in the same exercise. Again, no trucks.

On the third morning when Mother woke me up with the same alarming news, and yet again we were told the trucks were busy, I told her that I had had enough. No more of this stuff for me! I would not stay for another day.

"Where in the world do you want to go?" Mother asked.

"Why don't we go to the 'orphanage' that is under the protection of the Swedish government where Mary Hajós and her husband Emil are in charge?"

Mother was somewhat startled. "Do you think she would let us in after all you did to disturb her while she tried to lead Bible lessons in our home?"

"I am sure she would," I said. One of the qualities I had truly admired was her consistent kindness in spite of all my unfair behavior.

"But the orphanage is several kilometers away!" Mother exclaimed. "It is an island deep in the territory forbidden for Jews to walk through. We would look suspect during the day and even more so at night. It is an enormous risk, and the way things look, maybe these morning scares are just that – a harmless pastime for the local Arrow Cross men."

"Mom, I don't care. I will tear the yellow star off my coat, and I will be ready to go. We could stop over at our home and go on from there to Mary's."

Poor Mother stopped arguing. She never spent much effort on futile projects, and she knew it made no sense to try to convince me to stay.

We said nothing to the others. Promptly at 11:00 that morning as the curfew was lifted, we left the house with the stars on our coats held on only by a single thread. It was easy to tear them off. I jammed mine deep in my pants pocket.

I wonder what the two of us looked like. Certainly, we were filled with determination, but also with fear. If we had been caught, we would have been dragged into a local Arrow Cross headquarters, and a bullet would have been the least troublesome, most gentle death. The stories of tortures were rampant in those days.

Risky Journey

We made an effort to look relaxed. To look worried was Jewish.

We decided to make two stops on the way. Our first stop was the home of the Döblins, the janitor couple in the six-story apartment house at 23 Szemere Street where we had lived for the last ten years. This couple belonged to the minority whose moral sense was not blinded and who still saw us as people and not just as Jews.

They were truly frightened when we arrived. They ushered us into their small kitchen and treated us to coffee and a few cookies. We asked them if we could stay overnight in our apartment on the fifth floor if it was not yet occupied. We would then start out early in the morning to our destination across town.

Mrs. Döblin thought this was a bad idea considering the fact that most of the new tenants in the house were favorites of the Arrow Cross. They would be sure to report any unusual event or face in the house and that would be the end of both the Döblins and of us.

Oszkár Hajós's Home

Our next stop was the home where Mary and Emil Hajós used to live. Oszkár, Mary's brother-in-law, and the Rózsas, a Jewish-Christian couple, were minding the place under special protection of the Swedish government. We hoped they would be home when we arrived and that they would put us up for the night.

Our hearts were pounding as we knocked at the door, and to our great relief, Oszkár Hajós opened the door. We were welcomed with a simple but nourishing meal in an atmosphere filled with warmth, compassion, and under the circumstances, unexplainable confidence and cheer. We were taken in with some risk because, despite the Swedish plaque on the door, neighbors could have noticed and reported our presence. We were given a place to sleep and felt very much at home in this oasis in the war-torn jungle. Fortunately, the night was relatively calm with no bombings nearby. We were lulled to sleep by the comforting, increasing rumble of the approaching Russian artillery. In the morning, we learned that the room we had occupied was Oszkár's, a jovial man in his fifties. He had slept in the long bathtub in the bathroom.

After breakfast, Mother and I prepared to say farewell to our kind friends and to begin the several-kilometer journey to the "orphanage." Mrs. Rózsa was very concerned about our undertaking and asked if we would mind having her say a brief prayer before we departed. While I was not keen on participating in a prayer led by someone else, I could not refuse after having experienced the kindness and courage of those who hid us for the night.

As Mrs. Rózsa bowed her head and asked for God's closeness, guidance, and providence on our risky journey, I listened not only to her words but to the tone of confidence that indicated she believed that God was really present, that He listened and cared, and that He could truly influence the outcome of our effort. This prayer somehow created in me the impression that God could be right there as opposed to residing in a faraway kingdom, isolated from our daily activities and experiences. While I could not understand it all – nor did I really try – it gave me hope that God might just be keeping an eye on us as we made this trip.

This may have been the first time I had the sense that it could be possible to have real, direct communication with God.

On Our Way Again

We said farewell, and as we left on this cold, gloomy December morning, we could see in the eyes of our hosts their concern, wondering if they would ever see us again. I walked down the stairs with Mother, and we told each other not to let fear show on our faces, to walk with an air of confidence.

There was scattered shelling and the increasing sounds of machine guns. The sirens were silent because at this point we were in a permanent state of air raid. The only people on the streets were those who absolutely had to go somewhere. All others stayed in their air raid shelters day and night.

We avoided looking into people's eyes, afraid that we would betray our fear. Even more pressing, we watched for any sign of the armbands of the Arrow Cross troops. Whenever one appeared, if there was no way to avoid visual contact, we changed course or turned toward a shop window.

We were on Csengery Street when the shelling and bombing became so intense that the few people left walking on the street ran into buildings for shelter. We would have preferred to do the same except we were afraid that upon entering a building someone would ask us questions. We continued until shells began exploding around us at an alarming rate. Finally, we decided to seek cover in the entrance area of the next building. We opened the door and, to our horror, stepped into the beehive-like activity of armed Arrow Cross men in their dreaded uniforms. We were in one of the Arrow Cross section headquarters in which they interrogated, tortured, and murdered the Jews they captured, removing the corpses during the nights. There must have been sixty of these men in the small courtyard.

A uniformed man grabbed me by the collar and held me at arm's length. "Get out of here immediately! This place is not for civilians!"

He did not have to say it twice. Within seconds we were outside. I had a flash of thought to thank God for the escape.

After that, the heavy shelling became to us only a nuisance which we tried to ignore as we again attempted to reach our destination.

8

Tom

December 1944

Budapest

Swedish Flag

AFTER A half hour more, we were greeted by the happy colors of a large Swedish flag hanging off the corner of a building. Through the fearless efforts of Raoul Wallenberg, the Swedish diplomat who was working to save as many Jews as possible, the mansion had become a refuge for Jewish adults and children.

As I expected, Mary took us in with open arms without any sign of bitterness toward me for having so persistently disturbed her classes in our home. She was happy that we had made it to this fortress of protection. She placed the two of us in a room where about a dozen mothers and their children were staying.

Food

With food scarce, and at skyrocketing prices, only a few stores managed to remain open. Obtaining food was a real challenge. Mary acquired most of our provisions on her daily, dangerous forages to the marketplace.

Every morning after a brief time of song, scripture reading, and prayer, she donned the garb of a nurse – a veil attached to a cap with the Red Cross embroidered on the front – and set out to make her rounds. Not even a Nazi or Arrow Cross soldier would pick on a person in that uniform. It took a lot of courage to do what she did because not only was she not a nurse, but she was Jewish, and most likely did not have papers that would indicate she was a Gentile.

Wearing the cap, hiking boots, and carrying a sixty-pound backpack, Mary called on her acquaintances in food shops and collected anything salvageable. Old vegetables, stale bread crusts covered with mold she carried home to be processed by a team of people who could handle a knife.

Mary never returned empty-handed. She always left the place cheerfully as if each day she were embarking on a challenging adventure – which it truly was – clearly enjoying the fact that God had given her the opportunity of keeping all of us from starvation. Whenever she returned, her laughter and praise of God filled the house.

One of Mary's greater feats was the acquisition of a barrel of coleslaw. Two of us helped her roll the barrel from the grocery store a few blocks away into the kitchen.

During the toughest period, our only food was roughly two large spoonfuls of this coleslaw per day. We kept our little portion in a paper cup and picked out a few strands whenever our hunger got painful. Rinsing the cup clean for the next day became part of everyone's evening routine.

Tom – December 1944

Another cause for celebration was when, after a month of not a speck of meat touching our taste buds, Mary was given a skinny but whole chicken to feed her eighty "orphans." We had green pea puree with a tiny piece of chicken in the center of a small pool of gravy. Most of us ate the puree around the chicken first and, as the grand finale, treated ourselves to the chicken. We held it in our mouth and chewed it very slowly to prolong its pleasure.

I remember this so vividly! To this day, I marvel at the easy access we have to a hamburger at McDonald's. And whenever the family gets a side order of coleslaw at Kentucky Fried Chicken, I can't help but recall the joy of munching on coleslaw during the siege of Budapest. Since living through that experience, almost every meal appears like a feast, and seeing excess food thrown away burdens my conscience.

Another Close Call

One night around 10:00 as we were trying to fall asleep, we heard the dreaded banging at the front door. Mary was still in the kitchen taking the tea kettle off the stove. We heard her yelling, "Just a minute!" as she rushed to the door. We prayed like never before.

Later we found out what happened. She had opened the door and asked angrily, "What in the world are you up to this late? The last thing I need is for the children wake up and cause turmoil for hours! Looking at your worn-out faces, you should look for rest, not stirring up trouble. Your mothers would cry if they saw you in this shape! There is still some tea in the kettle. Sit down around the table. I have a few cookies. I'll read a verse from the Bible, say a brief prayer for you, and off you go!"

The bewildered group obeyed the feisty woman like a confused bunch of tamed wolves. While these Arrow Cross men sipped their tea and ate their cookies, Mary read from her Bible, "For God so loved the world that He gave His only begotten Son, that whoever believes in Him should not perish but have everlasting life."

Then she said a word of prayer for the worn-out bunch and for their families. She told them to leave and close the door very quietly so the children would stay asleep. The last one out patted her on the back with tears of thanks and puzzlement in his eyes.

The aftershock of this miracle was enough that Mary left the dishes undone. She lifted her eyes and thanked God for the deliverance, blew out the candle, and retired to her sleeping area without saying a word to the few who were still awake and anxious to find out what happened.

We found out about it in the morning when she prayed and thanked God that He had protected us and led away the people who had given us trouble the night before.

Tom – December 1944

I have realized since how close we may have been to the fate of others when the Arrow Cross searched even the buildings under Swiss or Swedish flags and then marched the Jews to the bank of the Danube to be shot, sending their bodies to a watery grave.

9
Tom
January 1945
Budapest

Devotions

DUE TO ever-increasing shelling from Russian cannons, life was gradually transferred to the basement. This was the site of daily morning and evening devotionals where Mary and Emil led the group in prayer, singing, and Bible exposition.

I avoided these devotionals by staying on the first floor by myself, going into the basement only when our meager meals were distributed. But one morning, after a bullet pierced the window and embedded itself in the wall close to where I was sitting, I retreated to the basement, descending the staircase in the dark and quietly sitting on a chair in the corner of the room. I refused to listen to any mention of the name of Jesus and was determined to sit perfectly still, keeping my ears as well as my mouth shut. I would have to endure this until the battle swept over and past us, and I could then be free from this exposure to a faith in which I had no interest.

Sitting in the dark room with the only light coming from a single candle that illuminated the Bible passage, it was difficult not to have my attention drawn to its flickering. As Mary spoke, I looked at the candle and occasionally would forget about my desire to be deaf to the message. A few words, and later, a few sentences reached my uninterested ears. Subconsciously, new thoughts began to develop in my mind that began to form a confusing puzzle.

Why was Mary Hajós so anxious to share her belief with me in spite of my obvious lack of desire?

What gave her the courage, or even a lack of respect for my privacy, to interfere with my life? I thought it was perfectly alright for her to make Christ and her Christian faith the main theme of her own life, but I resented her zeal to keep sharing it with all of us.

Dilemma

What I had great difficulty understanding and accepting was Mary's claim that one could be Jewish and believe in Jesus. In my mind, becoming Christian meant a breaking of ties with anything Jewish, including the sacredness and the teachings of the Hebrew Scriptures. I was convinced that the great and powerful God of Abraham, Isaac, and Jacob was good enough and all-sufficient for me. I did not need a middleman whose name I heard mostly associated with our persecution.

My image of Jesus was a kaleidoscopic one: the sweet baby with a halo around his head celebrated each year at Christmas; the sad, abused body hanging on the cross, his eyes lifted up to heaven in pain; and, finally, the fine-looking, supernatural, mythical, divine prince of the Hungarian Gentiles.

Jesus as the Messiah? I was expecting a radiant, powerful Messiah riding on a white horse who would finally restore our position as Jews in history. Instead, we saw him on hate posters. The picture was so devilishly skillful and horrid that it required significant maturity to ignore its message. For me, it created the impression that Jesus was the cause of our persecution.

I was certain that Jesus was the founder of a new religion in competition with and aimed against the one reflected in the Hebrew Scriptures. I believed that this was a plot to provide Gentiles with a new God who would claim superiority over the God of Abraham, Isaac, and Jacob. To my surprise, Mary and Emil used a Bible which contained both the Hebrew Scriptures and the New Testament. They quoted frequently from the Hebrew Scriptures and showed love and respect for it, but equally so for the New Testament.

Solution to the Puzzle

As I sat in that dark basement, I developed the ability to hear every quotation from the Hebrew Scriptures, and to ignore every quotation from the New Testament. The trouble started when the quotations from the Hebrew Scriptures revealed many thoughts and prophecies which were either unfamiliar to me or were in apparent conflict with the concept of Judaism itself. In my Jewish belief, there was no room for a special child to be born or for a son who would be called Prince of Peace. Yet, the book of Isaiah, chapter 9, verses 6 and 7, in my Hebrew Scriptures, contains these words:

For to us a child is born,
to us a son is given,
and the government will be on his shoulders;
And he will be called
Wonderful Counselor, Mighty God,
Everlasting Father, Prince of Peace.
Of the greatness of his government and peace
there will be no end.
He will reign on David's throne
and over his kingdom,
establishing and upholding it
with justice and righteousness
from that time on and forever.
The zeal of the Lord Almighty
will accomplish this.

It was strange to hear that the son would also be called "father" as if the two could coexist in a unified way. Surely it could not refer to the baby Jesus, born in Bethlehem, depicted by painters with a halo around his head.

Tom – January 1945

As to virgin birth, that clearly sounded like a Gentile fairy tale. It was disturbing to discover that it was mentioned in Isaiah 7:14:

Therefore the Lord Himself will give you a sign:
Behold a virgin will be with child and bear a son,
And she will call his name Immanuel.

As for the appearance and style of the Messiah, I was sure that he would be powerful, proud, and would march in pomp to the sound of trumpets. But Zechariah 9:9 predicts a different Messiah:

Behold your king is coming to you:
He is just and endowed with salvation,
Humble, and mounted on a donkey.

Isaiah 53:2-3 describes someone who

Has no stately form or majesty
That we should look upon him,
Nor appearance that we should be attracted to him.
He was despised and forsaken of men,
A man of sorrows and acquainted with grief;
And like one from whom men hide their face.
He was despised, and we did not esteem him.

Now why did all this happen to a mysterious future person? Isaiah 53:4-5 states:

Surely, our griefs he himself bore,
And our sorrows he carried;
Yet we ourselves esteemed him stricken,
Smitten of God, and afflicted.
But he was pierced through for our transgressions,
He was crushed for our iniquities;
The chastening for our well-being fell upon him,
And by his scourging we are healed.

Strange words from the Hebrew Scriptures: "He was pierced through..." One cannot help but think of the Jesus on the cross with his pierced hands and feet. "Crushed for our iniquities?" What sins would a twelve-year-old boy carry for which someone had to be hung? But, Isaiah 53:6 says,

All of us like sheep have gone astray and each of us turned to his own way.

Is it not sufficient to just lead a reasonably clean life doing good to ourselves and to others?

The more I listened, the more confused I became. These were all new concepts, and they came from my accepted authority, the Hebrew Scriptures. Of course, Mary and Emil read a good deal from the New Testament, too, but my well-adjusted ears and mind filtered all that out.

As I mused over these things, some New Testament verses started to trickle through. I asked Mary and Emil if the New Testament was written by Gentiles so the Gentiles would have their own scriptures. To my surprise, they explained to me that all the authors of the New Testament books were Jews with the possible exception of Luke. This was crucial information, which now made the New Testament as credible for me as what Mary called the "Old Testament." I began to explore it with respectful interest. I was intrigued by certain passages:

> *For all have sinned and have fallen short of the glory of God.* Romans 3:23.

> *For he who keeps the whole law, but fails in one point, has become accountable for all of it.* James 2:10.

> *If we say we have not sinned, we make Him a liar, and His word is not in us.* 1 John 1:10.

How about other sins? Did I never covet? How fully did I keep the famous Ten Commandments? Could it be that this sin – totally alien to a pure and perfect God –

could only be "paid for" by someone pure and completely righteous? Could that person be Jesus?

But, was Jesus really righteous? What was He like? What did He teach? If I wanted to find out more about Jesus, whether he was the Messiah or only pretended to be one, I had to dig into the New Testament. I borrowed a Bible from Mary and began to read it for myself.

It turned out to be interesting reading. I found no evidence of the rejection of Judaism or of the Hebrew scriptures. I found respect for Abraham, Isaac, Jacob, and the prophets, and the God of Jesus appeared the same as their God. If anything, I found that Jesus scolded Jews for not taking the Torah and the words of the prophets seriously enough. He scolded them for claiming to possess the Law while not putting the commandments into practice, and following their own will instead of following God.

At this point, I no longer had any illusions about my being a just person. I came to realize that I was a sinner and was not right in the sight of God. I could no longer miss paying attention to the powerful words in John 3:16:

> *For God so loved the world, that He gave His only begotten Son, that whoever believes in Him should not perish, but have everlasting life.*

Coming to Faith

On January 12, 1945, I came to the point where I did not know if Christianity and Jesus were, in fact, opposed to my Hebrew Scripture-based faith.

Could the New Testament, written predominantly by Jews, actually be Part II of the Hebrew Scriptures?

Could Jesus be the Messiah for whom we Jews were waiting?

I bowed my head in the pitch dark air raid shelter as I sat among the eighty-odd people who had settled down for another night of either peace or unexpected terror.

I turned to God saying, "God of Abraham, Isaac, and Jacob, I see that I am a sinner in your sight and need your forgiveness. Can you please help me to see clearly whether Jesus is really the Messiah? If He is, I want Him to become my Messiah, but if He is not, please help me to get rid of this confusion in my heart and mind. I am open to your answer, but please don't let me stay in this undecided state for too long."

I fell asleep that night with that prayer, sitting in my winter coat in the basement where there was no room for beds. I woke up the next morning with a strange feeling. Somehow the whole situation seemed clear.

As I thought about my question and prayer the night before, an unexplainable assurance swept over me, and I wondered how I could not have realized before this that

Jesus was really my Messiah. As if a veil had been lifted, somehow everything appeared different. In a way, I felt like a newborn.

I had to immediately share my discovery with some of the people around me. Some were sad to lose another stalwart Jewish ally to the "other side." Others embraced me because they had thought that I would never find what they had already discovered. Mother smiled and patted me on the back saying, "You see, it was really worth opening your mind to Christianity."

Although I am not sure that she had come to believe this for herself at the time, at least she could stop worrying about an open conflict developing between me and Emil and Mary as they led our devotional readings.

Mary was elated. I think she had been convinced that out of all those people, I was the only one not listening. She later said, "It was the biggest surprise that you were interested."

This was three days before my thirteenth birthday, a significant milestone in a Jewish boy's life. I remember putting down a few words in my diary, which marked the event simply but clearly: **"On this day of January 13, 1945, I accepted Jesus as my personal Savior and surrendered my life to God."**

10

Jutta

January 15, 1945

Puschkau, Poland

The Knock at the Door

WE WERE SITTING at dinner when we heard boots pounding up our front steps, then frantic knocking. When Mutti opened the door, I could see a boy, a little older than Walter. He had the belt with the black buckle that said "Blood and Honor." That meant he belonged to the Hitler Youth.

"Mrs. Merkel. You have to leave. NOW. The Russians are at the next village." Then he turned and pounded back down the steps.

Mutti came back to the table. "Walter, Jutta, go to your rooms. Put on two layers of clothes. Your gym pants, sweaters. We have to leave."

"Where are we going?" my brother asked.

"To the West."

"But I like Poland."

"I want to finish my sausage." I didn't like the feeling of Mutti's voice.

"There's no time, Jutta," she answered.

"I'm tired. I want to go to bed." Mutti ignored me.

"Bronja, bring me bread and some hard-boiled eggs." Bronja was our cook. She was Polish, and she was nice to us.

"Gisela, wake up Elke and Heidi. Dress them in their warmest clothes. Two layers."

My hands fidgeted at my belt as I stood up. My chest felt tight and playing with the buckle helped me feel better. The belt came off, and I swung it around in front of me and then over my head. The buckle whipped close to Mutti's face.

"Jutta. Put that down."

"But, Mutti, it makes me feel better."

"Go. And bring your school bags here."

I hopped out of the dining room and down the hall. I leaned on my dresser as I pulled out my wool stockings. Mutti had knitted them. They were horribly scratchy, but Mutti said to put on the warmest things. My gym pants had a smooth outer layer that would keep the snow from melting into the fuzzy lining. I sat on the bed while I pulled them on, then my cotton undershirt, then a pretty sweater Mutti had made me. I hopped over to the wardrobe and pulled out my heaviest sweater. I pulled it on over my head. Tipsi, my favorite doll, dressed in the red shorts and dark blue sweater Mutti had helped me knit, was sitting on my pillow. I picked her up as I swung my school knapsack over my shoulder.

Jutta – January 15, 1945

"Tipsi, we have to go. To the West," I whispered. I cradled her as I hopped back to the dining room.

Mutti was there already dressed in her sweater, coat, and her gray cape. She wore her nurse's cap with the pin with the red cross. Why she was wearing her uniform?

The dishes and the tablecloth were gone. Walter was handing Mutti his school knapsack. She poured the books out onto floor.

"But, Mutti, I want to take them," he said.

Bronja came in with a basket full of lumpy dish cloths. I smelled bread. One of the dish cloths was full of hard-boiled eggs.

Mutti waved at Bronja's basket. "Walter, Jutta. Fill up your knapsacks."

Mutti paused as Gisela, our governess from Berlin, arrived carrying Heidi, my three-year-old sister. Heidi was crying, asking Gisela to read to her. Elke came after her. She was crying about wanting to go back to bed.

"Gisela, get a baby blanket from Heidi's room. Jutta, put on your coat and get your boots."

I laid Tipsi on the table and hopped over to the closet, pulled my coat off its hanger, and dragged my boots over to a chair. I laced my boots all the way up. I stood on one foot while I pulled on my coat.

Gisela came back a minute later. Mutti took the blanket and wrapped it around me, over a shoulder and under my other arm. She knotted it at my shoulder and then lay Tipsi in the folds against my chest.

"Tipsi will be safe there," she said.

I peeked into the blanket and smoothed the folds under her. "I'll take care of you," I whispered.

The air stung. The snow was like the feathers that came out of a little hole in my pillow. I would blow them around my room and try to catch them. But these flakes weren't fun, and it was cold.

Gisela helped me onto the sled and set Heidi between my legs. The sled creaked as Gisela got it moving. Elke held her hand. Walter was bent over by a bag hanging around his neck. I had seen Bronja filling it with the silverware. Why were we taking the silver if we were leaving our dinner?

Before now, this sled had meant fun. We played with our friends, sliding down the hill by our house or pulling each other across the ice. Sometimes Gisela or Mutti pulled us on the way to the store.

Two days ago, Gisela and I had gone to the village to get some milk and cottage cheese. She had pulled me on this sled. I thought I heard thunder except you don't usually have thunder in the winter. Gisela said it was the Russian cannons that were somewhere out there to the east.

When the grown-ups were whispering, I sometimes I heard them talk about the Russians. They didn't like them, and I shivered when I heard Gisela's answer. They were some of our enemies.

When we lived at Schloss Parken, Walter and I used to listen at the keyhole of the living room when the adults were talking about the war. Sometimes I asked Walter about it. He didn't know any more than I did, but it helped to talk.

We thought that Hitler was going to take care of us, that none of our enemies could hurt us, and that we would rule the world. But no one was happy about the war now. Even my grandmother was quiet about it. She said Hitler was the best leader anyone could ever want, that everything was going to come out right because of him, and that he'd show the world that we Germans were better than everyone else.

It wasn't far to the train station, but it was slow going with the fresh snow and the weight of the sled. I wished I could walk.

11

Jutta

August – December 1944

Puschkau, Poland

Posen, Poland

Thorn

THE PROBLEM with my foot had started five months before. In August, I had been playing "catch me" with my best friend, Brigitte. There were beautiful pink rose bushes on the edges of our yard, and some of their branches sprawled across the grass. I knew how it felt to step on a thorn. I remember running on the side of my foot crying, "Mutti, Mutti, my foot hurts."

It had to be a thorn, but usually Mutti could pull thorns right out. This time, she couldn't see anything, and she got worried.

All I knew was that my foot hurt. It got worse every day. After a week, it was so bad I couldn't walk. Mutti was a nurse, but she didn't know what it could be. That's when she took me to the hospital. We had to take the train to Posen.

The doctor poked and pushed on it. I tried not to scream. He made me lie on a table, and he moved a machine over my foot. He told me to lie still. Mutti said that the machine was taking an x-ray, which would show the inside of my foot. It didn't show a thorn or anything else unusual. The doctor decided it was bone cancer. He said that I had to stay in the hospital for treatment. The doctor also pointed out that Mutti already had her hands full, working at the military hospital and taking care of my brother and two sisters.

Mutti didn't want to leave me, but she thought the doctor could help.

"Mutti, when will you come back?" I asked.

"I'll come when I can. Be a good girl. Remember your manners. You will get better here."

I cried when she left. I was scared that I wouldn't see her again.

I tried to be brave when Mutti visited. I didn't want to make life harder. She was already doing so much, and Vati was somewhere in the world helping with the war.

There in the hospital, I cried myself to sleep a lot of nights. I knew she couldn't hear me, but I was calling to her, "Mutti, Mutti, when am I going to see you again?"

One time, the nurse heard me. "Stop sniveling. That's enough of you feeling sorry for yourself. I had a pretty bad childhood, too. Crying isn't going to make it any better."

I made sure she didn't see me cry after that.

Once she said that I needed some fresh air. She wheeled my bed onto the balcony. It was a sunny day, and at first it was nice to be out of the smell and away from the cries of the other patients. But it was cold. I had only my hospital gown and one thin blanket. I could not stop shivering. I sobbed and screamed, but no one saw me or heard me. I thought I was going to freeze to death.

The nurse finally brought me back inside. It took me until the next day before I got warm again.

Almost every night, we would hear the siren that said that planes were coming. Then two men would put me on a stretcher and carry me down to the basement. All of the other patients were there, too. The next plane could drop a bomb, and we could be dead in a minute. We all breathed again when the siren sounded the tone that told us that it was safe to go upstairs.

The food was awful. I especially couldn't stand the soup. It was thin and had pieces of pumpkin sitting on the bottom. It tasted like it might have been made with vinegar. We had it almost every day. We also got bread, but it wasn't like what we had at home. Bronja was a good cook and only made things we liked.

In November, a Polish boy about my age moved into my room. His mother visited him a few times. She always brought him a sausage and one for me, too. I ate it slowly to keep the taste in my mouth as long as I could.

The fish was gray and watery and tasted like the water I had swallowed when we went swimming in the river. The boy didn't like the fish either. We made up a game. If we pushed on the edge of our plates, we could make the fish fly across the room. Whoever flipped their fish the farthest was the winner.

The other rooms were full of soldiers. All of them had bandages – on their shoulders, legs, arms, heads, or all over their bodies. Sometimes they would moan. Some of them cried when the nurse walked past, but she didn't pay any attention. I wished I could help.

One of the soldiers who could walk and use his hands told me I reminded him of his sister. He asked me if I liked dolls. Dolls had always been my favorite playmates. The soldier made me a dollhouse out of cardboard. It had rooms and little furniture. He cut out a couple of dolls, too. They were my friends, and they invited me to play with them in their house.

Sometimes I could hear rumbles and bangs in the distance. I didn't know what it was. The Polish boy thought it was the war, but he didn't know anything more than that. When it was getting closer to Christmas, I could even see lights flashing.

Just before Christmas, Mutti came to the hospital to take me home. She was getting me dressed when the doctor came in.

"I cannot allow you to take her. She will be a great burden to you and your other three children. If the war gets too close, I will put her on a train made especially for the hospital. Our enemies will know that it is full of sick patients, and they will let us go. Can you protect her like that?"

Mutti told him, "I am a nurse at the military hospital in Puschkow. The soldiers say that the battles are not going well. The army is getting pushed back. The Russians are advancing."

"You should know better than to listen to them. They are making excuses for themselves. We will win this war. We are better than the Russians. Hitler has a plan."

He kept yelling, but Mutti ignored him and finished getting me dressed.

"How are you going to get her home? You are an irresponsible, sentimental woman. You should be ashamed, putting her into more danger than if she stayed here."

But Mutti didn't answer him. She pulled me onto her back. She carried me out of the building and down the street to the train station. I kept slipping off because of her fur coat, but she just hoisted me back up.

I was so happy to be home. My sisters had grown a lot in the five months I was gone. Bronja's food was wonderful, and Tipsi was waiting for me.

On New Year's Day, only two weeks ago now, I was sitting in bed drawing on my slate. The red sore on my foot was oozing and bleeding. That wasn't new, but this time I saw a hard, brown spot pushing up.

"Mutti, Mutti, something is poking up out of my foot."

She got the tweezers from her nurse's bag and pulled at it. A long, fat thorn came out. It had been in there for five months. It had gone in at the bottom of my foot and was coming out of the top.

After that, I started to be able to put some weight on my foot. Gisela had been helping me learn to walk. She would hold my hands and back up as I worked on shifting my weight to my bad foot. It still hurt, but it was getting better.

12

Jutta

January 1945

Puschkau, Poland

Posen, Poland

Czechoslovakia

Trains to Dresden

WE WEREN'T the only ones coming to the train station. The platform was mobbed with mothers and grandmothers and children. Everyone looked scared. Some of the children were crying and pulling away from their mothers. The mothers were screaming at them saying they might be left behind if they didn't stay close.

One woman saw Mutti's uniform. She cried for her to find her daughter. Mutti said she was sorry, but she had her own four children to take care of. I knew Mutti would protect us, but I was shaking. I could feel the fear all around us.

The train finally pushed into the station. We all had to step back out of the way of the engine. Then everyone tried to get in at the same time. There were already people on the train, and now it was filling up fast. We weren't even near the door. Mutti said something to Gisela and then left us and pushed her way into the train. She was carrying Heidi.

"Mutti! Where are you going?" we screamed.

Then we saw her inside the train. She worked at a window and got it open. Gisela picked me up and pushed me through. I landed on two people, but I didn't care. I was just happy to be inside with Mutti. Elke fell in next. And then Walter. He crawled up into the luggage net above our seats. The train started moving. We were in, but where was Gisela? Then I saw her pushing her way down the aisle toward us.

A lot of people were still on the platform.

"Mutti, will there be another train for them?" I asked.

"I don't know, Jutta. I don't think so, but I don't know," Mutti answered.

"What's going to happen to them?" I was drowned out with the crying around me.

"Nurse! Nurse! Can you help me?" A woman called Mutti. She was carrying a boy whose face was bleeding. I couldn't see what Mutti did, but the woman looked happier.

There was a lady with a girl about my age. The girl was crying. Her legs were stiff and white.

"Mutti, what's wrong with her legs?" I asked.

"They're frozen," she said. I had felt cold before, but not like that.

"Mutti, I'm hungry." This time it was Walter. I was, too.

"Eat a piece of bread, but not much," she answered.

"Nurse! Nurse!" This time the person calling was down at the other end of the car. Mutti started to move toward the voice.

"Mutti, don't go," I cried.

Mutti called back, "Stay in your seats. I'll be back in a minute."

The girl with the frozen legs was watching while I ate my bread. I broke my piece in half and gave her some. Her mother opened her bag and pulled out my favorite – Ganze Schmalz – goose lard on bread. She gave me a piece. Before I ate it, I asked Tipsi if she wanted some. She said she did. I heard the woman who gave it to me tell Mutti that I must really love my doll that I take such good care of her. That made me feel good.

They made all of us get off at Posen. They said that the partisans were going to blow up the train. Mother explained that partisans were Polish people who didn't like us Germans and were trying to hurt us.

Mutti asked about a train to Dresden. That is where my Tante Tutti and Onkel Werner and my cousins, Hannelore, and Christian lived. The man said that there wouldn't be another train until the next day.

We said goodbye to Gisela there in Posen. She was going on another train that would take her to Berlin. She was worried whether her family would still be there. She looked scared when she left us.

She had been assigned to us by the government in its program to provide help to families with many children. She had been with us for more than a year. She was only a few years older than I, but she had been like another mother when Mutti was away at work.

We spent the rest of that night in the station. I tried leaning against a post, but my foot was hurting more. Mutti lifted me up onto a window sill. It was just wide enough to be able to lie down. I put my knapsack under my head and decided to pretend that I was in my own room. I was too cold and scared to sleep very much. At least Tipsi was warm and safe in her blanket.

Walter's stomach was hurting. He screamed and cried the whole night. Mutti tried to help him, but he couldn't calm down.

The next day, we got onto another train. Mutti said it was going to Czechoslovakia, but then we would go on to Dresden. The people were a little quieter on this train.

Mutti was able to sit down for a while. She had tears running down her cheeks. I had never seen her cry. I asked if I could help. She said she wished Vati could be with us. I missed him, too.

Everything was quiet until we saw the sparks. The branches on either side of us were full of little fires. Everyone started screaming. Some said that we needed to go back. Others yelled at them that we can't go back because of the Russians. I was scared by both ideas. The train kept going. We got through the woods without catching on fire.

We stopped at a little station. Someone came onto the train and told us we had to get off, that the tracks ahead had been blown up. The station had some walls, but bombs had destroyed the roof. There wasn't anywhere to sleep except outside on the platform.

When the sky was getting lighter, we woke up to someone screaming and pointing at something on the ground. They said that it was a bomb that was still alive. We got away from it as fast as we could.

That day, we got onto another train that was using good tracks. There was one more stop before we finally got to Dresden. It was in a city in Czechoslovakia. We had to get off because the right train wasn't going to come until the next day. We were standing in the station when a German officer came over to us. Mutti told him that we needed to spend the night and asked if he knew of anywhere the five of us could stay. The man led us to a hotel, at least that is what the sign said. Part of it was ruined and most of the windows were shattered. He showed us some rooms that had not been bombed. We slept there that night.

My foot had gotten better during our travels, and I wasn't hopping any more. I couldn't walk fast, but I was using both feet.

13

Jutta

January-February 1945

Dresden, Germany

Dresden

TANTE TUTTI was Mutti's sister. We hadn't seen her, Onkel Werner, and my cousins for a year. Ever since we had moved to Poland, we had only seen them at Christmas at my Onkel Biller and Tante Britta's, but they hadn't come this year, probably because of the war.

My cousin, Hannelore, was almost the same age as I. Her brother, Christian, was a little younger. We always played together with our other cousins when they came for Christmas. It was usually a lot of fun, but when we last saw each other, Hannelore was mean. I think she was mad because our grandmother, Omi, was also my godmother. My bed was in Omi's room, and sometimes she gave me special treats.

One day, Hannelore started a fight with me. She told Omi that I bit her. Omi thought I was lying when I said that Hannelore had started it. Omi gave me a beating on the backs of my legs with a willow switch. It hurt a lot.

There in Dresden, I was remembering that time, but we didn't talk about it. I was just glad to be in a warm house with people who were taking care of us.

On some of the nicer days, Onkel Werner and Tante Tutti took us to the zoo. I had never been to a zoo and had only seen pictures of the animals we saw there. I especially liked watching the silly monkeys. The lions, snakes, and elephants were scary.

I loved Onkel Werner. Mutti said that he was a lawyer and a judge. He must have been stern in his work, but he had a sweet disposition with us. He made us feel very welcome. The zoo was one of his favorite places, second only to the train station. Before the war, he knew every train and train schedule by heart. During the war, the trains could not be trusted to be on time, or even whether they would arrive on the right days.

Walter and I went to the school near their house. I didn't learn anything because almost every day the air raid sirens would go off right when we were taking out our slates. We would throw our coats back on and run home. Then we would stay in the cellar with the rest of the family until the sirens made the long steady tone that said it was clear to come out. It was usually too late to go back to school.

When we were in the air raid shelter, we could hear the planes flying low. Sometimes we could hear the bombs. I would put my fingers in my ears so that I would not hear them. I remembered when I was little when we lived in Berlin. We had to run to the cellar whenever we heard the sirens. I was so scared that Mutti couldn't get my hands off my ears. I was older now, but I was just as scared. I didn't let it show like I did when I was little.

One night when we were in the cellar, Mutti said, "Tutti, it's not safe here. We are going to leave tomorrow."

"You're crazy. You're in Germany. Hitler won't let the enemies get into our country. We will win the war."

"We're leaving tomorrow."

Tutti started yelling. "You can't leave. I won't let you go out there and be killed by these bombs."

Mutti didn't answer.

"Where do you think you'll go? Where will you be safer?"

I was scared. What was Mutti thinking? I didn't want to go back out in the cold. I wanted to go home, but I knew better than to say anything.

Mutti had told us that we couldn't go back to Berlin because the house we lived in had been bombed just a few months after we had moved to Poland. Mutti saw it when she went back to give birth to Heidi. She said that there were only piles of wood and stones. She had looked through the rubble, and all she had found was a little pot from my dollhouse.

The day after her argument with Tante Tutti, we got dressed in all of our warm clothes again. Tante Tutti still thought that Mutti was wrong to leave and that we would be in more danger, but they weren't fighting about it this time.

I knew Mutti would take care of us.

14

Jutta

February 1945

Aue, Germany

Aue

MY OTHER GODMOTHER, Frau Lose, lived in the mountains near Dresden in a town called Aue. She and her husband had good positions at the Wellner Silver factory. The bag that Walter carried was full of silver tableware from them.

We were with Frau Lose for about a month, but we spent a lot of the time in their bomb shelter. Its walls were foot-thick cement. It was the biggest house in the area and lots of neighbors were in the shelter with us. We even spent some of the nights sleeping in the bunk beds down there.

The house was set into a mountain, and there was a door that looked out toward Dresden. We could look out through a hole in the door.

One day, I was sitting on a bed playing with Tipsi. Walter was at the peephole.

"Jutta, come here!"

I ran over to him and looked out. There were airplanes flying down in the valley. They were in triangle formations lined up behind and beside each other. They came in waves, covering the sky every few minutes. We could hear the droning of their engines.

"So many of them." We wanted to count them, but they spread out all the way to the horizon.

"There goes Dresden," said one of the adults.

That scared me. What about Tante Tutti and Onkel Werner? Were Hannelore and her brother all right? I wished they had come with us. Mutti was right about leaving.

During the first night after we saw the planes, we saw little flashes of red. The next nights, it looked like a sunset glowing with red and orange. Even during the day, the clouds over the city were red. Someone said that they weren't clouds. It was smoke, and the city was burning.

When the airplanes stopped coming, we couldn't see the city any more. The valley was only smoke. A few days later, when we looked out, the smoke was gone, but we couldn't see any of the tall buildings. One of the men said that our enemies had bombed the whole city.

It was starting to be spring when we left Frau Lose's house. Mutti said we were going south to Austria. I was scared of leaving, but Mutti said we couldn't stay with Frau Lose any longer. She said that the Austrians were not in the war in the same way as Germany.

Mutti said we would be safe.

15

Jutta

March 1945

Bregenz, Austria

Bregenz

ONKEL WERNER had a friend, Dr. Koch in Bregenz, Austria. They were members of an organization, a 'brotherhood,' of lawyers and judges. Mutti told us that our enemies were not bombing Austria.

Onkel Werner must have gotten word to Dr. Koch because he welcomed us. He had a big house in the city overlooking Lake Constance. It was quiet there, and we didn't have to live in an air raid shelter.

Walter got sick with diphtheria while we were there. He had to go to the hospital so that the rest of us would not catch it. I was worried about him. I knew what a hospital was like, and I didn't want him to go through that.

Two days after he went to the hospital, we heard a knock at the door. Walter was standing there in his striped pajamas with his school knapsack on his back.

He was crying. "Mutti, Mutti, don't take me back. I'll live outside in the chicken coop, but don't take me back."

He had escaped from the hospital and had walked through the city to Dr. Koch's house. He told me later that he was afraid we would move away without him.

Mutti let him stay.

16

Jutta

April 1945

Schwartzenberg, Austria

Move to Dikach

I DON'T know why we couldn't stay at Dr. Koch's. It was a beautiful house with a wonderful living room. I had started to feel better, not as scared all the time, but now we had to move again. Mutti said that Dr. Koch was taking us to his friends in the mountains. They knew of a house where we could live.

Dr. Koch drove us up winding roads to the village of Schwartzenberg. It was surrounded by mountains with jagged gray peaks. There were green forests climbing up their sides. There was still snow on the ground, but snowdrops were poking through the thinner patches.

Dr. Koch left us with the Kofler family. They welcomed us into their home, and we stayed with them for a few days. Then we moved into a house that was in a little valley a mile outside the village. The valley was called Dikach. Mr. Kofler said that the house had been occupied by displaced workers from the Ukraine, but they had left a few weeks before we came.

It was a comfortable, wooden farmhouse surrounded by woods and fields. We settled in and finally started to feel like we had a home. We didn't have to fear the

Russians. There were no airplanes flying over. There were no bombs here, and we didn't have to live in a cellar. The people were not thinking about the war all the time.

In the next few months, flowers bloomed in the fields all around our house. It was so much prettier than in Poland. There, the flowers grew in gardens, but here, flowers were everywhere. We picked bouquets for Mutti to arrange in a vase for our table. She also taught me how to make crowns by weaving the flowers together. I made them for my sisters and for myself and for my friends.

The house had a room upstairs where two of us had beds. It was a lovely room except that bedbugs would gather together for a conference on the ceiling over my bed. Every night, they would see me coming and would send the order to attack. They would drop on me like thumbtacks. Mutti would pick them off with a needle and burn them in the flame of a candle. The bugs were not interested in anyone else in the family.

In the evenings, we sometimes sat around the black stove and sang. Walter had an especially beautiful voice. We remembered German folk songs. We five made our own choir, feeling cozy and warm as we sang around the stove.

Tipsi was my constant playmate. I loved playing mother. She was my only child and was very real to me. When she disobeyed, I scolded her.

17
Jutta
1936-1942
Berlin, Germany

Early Years

MY DOLL had been a Christmas gift from Onkel Bamann when I was four. We were living in Berlin then. Mutti had a friend named Tipsi, and I always liked her name. The doll was the size of a real baby, but she looked more like a little girl. Her clothes were more like mine than a baby's.

Christmases in Berlin were warm and wonderful. Christmas Eve was an exciting day. We were never allowed to see the Christmas tree until then. It was set up in the Herrenzimmer, Vati's special living room, and was decorated with real candles and shiny tinsel icicles. Gifts surrounded the tree. We would run in and find the ones with our names on them. Later, after we had played with our gifts, we would stand in a circle around the tree and sing "Silent Night." Mutti and Vati had beautiful voices. All of us together sounded like a choir.

The Herrenzimmer was off limits to Walter, Elke, and me on every other day of the year. There was once, though, that Vati let us come in. He had a map on the wall with little red flags stuck into it. He said they were marking where our army was fighting. I wanted to play with them, but he told me not to touch them.

One afternoon when Vati was not home and Walter was engrossed in his train set – he protected it like a raw egg and did not let me even come near it – I snuck into the Herrenzimmer and pulled a chair over to the map. The little flags came out easily. I got down off the chair and arranged them in circles and triangles on Vati's desk.

That's when he got home from work. I heard him before he found me in his room. I ran, but the flags were still on his desk. He found me and asked if I had played with the flags. I said it wasn't me, but he didn't believe me. He spanked me hard. It hurt, but I knew I had lied to him. I knew I deserved the spanking.

After I went to my room, I decided that I didn't want to live there anymore. I told Mutti I was leaving. She showed sadness. She asked what I thought I would need to take along. She gave me a basket, packed some rolls with butter and marmalade, a bottle of water, some apples, toothpaste, a toothbrush, and a small towel. She gave me a warm, parting hug.

There was a bench on the other side of a field in our neighborhood where I wanted to sit and think.

As I was walking through the field, I heard an angry man shouting to people in a nearby sports arena.

A neighbor was in the field picking strawberries. "Where are you going?" she asked me.

"I don't know, but I'm not going home."

"Do you think your parents would like some strawberries? You could drop them off at your house and then be on your way."

I thought, "My parents don't deserve strawberries," but I was willing to take her hand and walk back across the field.

Mutti and Vati welcomed me home. Vati assured me of his love and forgiveness, and Mutti asked me to think it over one more time before I left for good. They hugged me and made me feel better about staying home. I gracefully obliged to give up my plan.

Walter was no angel either. There was a black wrought iron gate between our house and the street. Mutti would hang an empty bag on the gate to be filled by the baker's son as he made the daily rounds on his bicycle. One day, Mutti found the bag empty. She thought something had gone wrong for the baker, but she discovered that Walter was to blame. He had stolen peach jelly and butter from the pantry, taken the bag of rolls, and invited his friends to join him for breakfast. I envied his ability to get away with such pranks with only a scolding!

Our home in Berlin was a comfortable, old house in a nice neighborhood. Most of the rooms had dark woodwork and dark wallpaper, but my parents made it a nice home. There were flowers, Gänseblümchen, in the yard all around the house. Walter and I would pick them and bring little bouquets to the neighbors. We gave some to Mutti to put on our table.

Walter and I played with children who lived in the neighborhood. Walter and his friends pretended they were soldiers in the war. Vati made him an army uniform just like his own. He even had a helmet and a toy machine gun. My friends and I played with our dolls. We would put them in a baby carriage and take them out for walks or send them off to school with little backpacks with miniature slates stuffed inside. We sometimes played that we needed to escape from the war.

One day when I was three, Vati brought home two turtles. He put up a fence around a tree in our backyard for them to live in. We named them Lotte and Liese and brought them lettuce leaves and celery every day. We enjoyed watching them eat and waddle around their yard.

One day when we came out with their lunch, they were lying still with swarms of ants crawling over them. We didn't know if the ants had killed them or if they had died first and the ants came afterward. We had a lovely funeral and buried them in the yard.

When men came to visit Vati, they would sit in the Herrenzimmer in the brown leather chairs and smoke and talk. Walter and I would peek at them through the keyhole. We heard them talk about Germany. I knew that Hitler was our Führer and that Germany was going to rule the world. I also knew that we hated the Jews. There were posters all over the city that made them look evil and scary. If we were noisy, Mutti would tell us to be quiet and not be like Jews, or if Walter forgot to take his hat off, Mutti scolded him saying "Take off your hat. This isn't a Jewish school."

There were flags all over the city, red and white with a black spider design in the middle. They were draped down the fronts of important buildings, and they were flying in front of a lot of peoples' houses. I didn't think much about them until two men in the gray uniforms came to our door and asked Vati why there was no flag on our house. Vati said that they cost too much. *(Looking back, I don't think that was the issue.)*

"No problem, Mr. Merkel. We will give you one as a present. Tomorrow you will proudly hang it on your house."

After that, we had one of those flags by our door.

Vati was a weapons specialist for the German army. He taught at the military academy. He often wasn't home for dinner. On those nights, our Croatian maid, Anka, would set his dinner aside and warm it up when he got home.

I had just turned four when our enemies started bombing our city. Whenever we heard the sirens, we would grab our knapsacks and the warm clothes that were always at the foot of our beds and run downstairs. Our cellar became the air raid shelter for our neighbors as well.

We played with the other children except when we heard the airplanes flying over and bombs exploding. I was so scared. It always took me a while to be able to play again.

After the siren said it was safe, we would run upstairs and get the wooden cigar boxes that Vati had given us. Then we hurried outside to find the best bits of shrapnel. Our favorites were the shiniest and biggest pieces. We put them in the boxes and then compared our treasures with those of our friends. Sometimes we traded with them to add to our collections. There were also little strips of silver metal that we saved to become wonderful ornaments for our Christmas tree.

I had just turned six when Vati left. We didn't know he was leaving except that one afternoon he gathered us in the living room and gave each of us a hug. We didn't see him the next day. Mutti said that he was being sent somewhere to help the war effort and that he would be back soon.

Vati never told Mutti where he was going. She watched him pack the white uniform with the short pants. Since Japan was the only warm country who was on our side, she guessed that he was going there. Her guess was confirmed when she went with him to the train station. The conductor was not supposed to announce the destinations of the trains, but he did this time. The train was going to Bordeaux, the port for ships heading to Japan.

18

Jutta

May-August 1945

Dikach, Austria

End of the War

IT HAD BEEN a few years since Vati went away. While we were running from the Russians and were so afraid, we wished he were with us to protect us. Here in Austria, we still missed him, but usually we felt quite safe.

An exception was on one of the days in May. Walter and I were walking across a field on our way home from the village. It was quiet and birds were singing. Then we heard a low buzzing. Walter recognized it before I did.

"Jutta, get down!"

He threw me into a ditch and fell on top of me. The plane flew over, shooting the ground as it came. Bullets landed all around us. We were both shaking when we dared to get up.

I realized afterward that if they had hit us, Walter would have died, and I would have been protected. I am still grateful for such a brave and loving brother.

One afternoon, we saw troops filling the roads and racing across the open fields. Within a few hours, a black man in a French uniform knocked at our door. He wanted to know if there were any German soldiers in the house. He checked every room with his gun ready and then left without saying a word.

Mutti said, "Well, children, this must be the end of our part of the war. Don't panic, we'll see what the future will bring. Just make sure you stay inside the house!"

None of us knew what to think or what to say. It did not sink in that our invincible country could be defeated. That evening, Mutti prepared the simple dinner we had gotten used to. We didn't say much to each other as we got ready for bed. It was like we were holding our breath to see what would happen next.

Soon after that, two French soldiers came to our door. They were looking for jewelry, gold watches, butter, and alcohol. Mutti told them that we had nothing that they wanted. Amazingly, they believed her and left.

Another day, a soldier asked Walter for directions to the village of Andelsbuch. He offered to give Walter a cigarette if he would show him the way. Mutti sent me with Walter. We walked with him down the path to the river. There was a wooden box on the bank attached to a rope above the river. We always used it on our way to the village. Walter showed him how to sit in the box and pull himself across the river above the wild current. The man gave Walter the cigarette, but I didn't see him smoke it.

Our fear of the soldiers and the war gradually disappeared. We relaxed into a warm family life filled with making handicrafts, singing German folk songs, and keeping the little house clean and cheery. When we had flour, sugar, butter, and eggs, we would make a cake, taking turns stirring the batter with a spoon that had a hole in it.

I loved playing with Tipsi on the warm bench that surrounded the tile stove. I started to relax and even enjoy our exile.

On one of the days, we all hiked to Dornbirn, a larger village down toward the lake. Mutti bought hats for Elke, Heidi, and me. Mine was navy blue with a little flower on the brim. She said that they were Tyrolean and were a traditional Austrian style. They would keep the sun off our faces.

Another time we went swimming with our new friends in a lake created by a dam. There were turbines turning the water pressure into electricity. I was not a good swimmer, and if it weren't for Walter and our friends dragging me out of the current, I would have been swept into the whirlpool made by the water heading downward to the turbines. I have never liked deep water since then.

Our Austrian neighbors offered us food and clothes. One of our friends made a wonderful dress for me from a sheet. She decorated it with a ribbon around the hem

Mutti always seemed to find food for us. We knew that sometimes she would ask our neighbors if they could spare some eggs, milk, or other essentials. We didn't call it begging, but we were dependent on others.

We had a wonderful surprise! Tante Tutti, Onkel Werner, Hannalore, and Christian came to visit. They were staying in Bregenz with Dr. Koch. We hiked through the valleys and on the mountain trails. I was glad my foot was healed so that I could hike with everyone.

They told us that a few days after we had left Dresden, their house had been bombed. The second floor where we had our bedrooms had been demolished. They said that the city was burning when they escaped. It was so hot that the soles of their shoes burned off. They got away just before their feet would have been badly burned. I was so glad they made it out in time.

They also told us that the bombs had hit the zoo, and the animals became loose in the city. They didn't see any of them, but they had heard that they all died in the fires. I tried not to think about it, but I couldn't help but imagine the cute monkeys swinging through the trees in the city. It was a nice thought until I remembered that the trees would have been on fire.

Mutti had known it was time to leave Dresden. If we had stayed even a few days more, we would have been hit by the bomb that destroyed the house. I realized that when we lived in Poland, she had known we would need to escape from the advancing Russian army when she rescued me from the hospital, even before the Hitler youth had knocked at our door. If we had stayed even a few hours longer, we would have missed the last train. At the station, she had figured out how to get ahead of the crowd by pushing us through the window onto the train. After Dresden and Aue, she knew to take us far away from the bombs to the beautiful mountains of Austria.

Near the end of the summer, Mutti was told that we could continue to live in Austria if we would become Austrian citizens. The people would continue to take care of us, and we would have a house to live in. As nice as it sounded, Mutti did not consider it for long. We were German, and Austria would never be home.

We were on the move again.

19
Jutta
September 1945 – Spring 1946
Oberstaufen, Germany

Return to Germany

A FARMER CAME with his pickup truck and loaded us and our belongings into its open bed. We were sad and worried about having to leave our home in Austria, but we expected that we would be able to settle more permanently in our own country. The farmer was taking us to the closest crossing into Germany, a bridge over the Eibelebach, the river that was the border between the two countries.

When we arrived at the river, we discovered that the bridge had been destroyed. Boards, one for each set of wheels, had been lain down in its place. I closed my eyes and held my breath while the driver inched the truck along. A wiggle in either direction would have sent us down into the raging river. Somehow, he got us safely to the other side.

He dropped us off at a building that had once been a hotel and restaurant. There was a beautiful door with a welcoming sign: "Grüss Gott." ("Good Day") I hoped that it would be good.

We unloaded our belongings into a large room that had been the restaurant dining room. Chairs were upside down on the tables. For the first few nights, we slept on the floor among the cobwebs and dust. I cleaned out a corner and made a cozy space for Tipsi and me. Then we moved upstairs into two small rooms. The windows of the hotel had been broken and many were missing. When winter came and it turned cold, snow blew into some of the rooms. I scraped ice off the inside of the windows with my fingernail.

We had a small, black wood stove for warmth, but we had no wood, nor money to purchase some. Instead, we went out to the woods to collect what we could find, but it was never enough. It burned quickly, and we were usually cold. There were times when I could not stop shivering.

On one of the cold days, Mutti sent me to find some wood. I thought it was not fair that the owners, a family who lived on the first floor, had a well-stocked wood pile while we were freezing. I decided that they would not miss a few logs.

The daughter of the family saw me. "Jutta, what are you doing there?"

"We're freezing."

"That's not our problem. Put that back."

I went back to Mutti without anything. I think she went out into the woods herself to find more wood.

Walter would cry about being hungry. "Mutti, I have such a hunger. Don't you have even a tiny corner of bread for me?" Sometimes we had only one meal for the day. We trusted that Mutti would keep us from starving to death, but we noticed that there were many meals when she ate nothing. Mutti visited our neighbors when we had nothing left. Sometimes she came back with a few pieces of bread. When she did, we often had bread soup: pieces of bread torn up and cooked in milk. Occasionally, she would get a little meat which she would use to make soup.

The family who lived below us were farmers. The father of the family was kinder than his wife and oldest daughter. He would allow Walter and me to help with the animals – cows, chickens, and geese. He gave us the job of shoveling out the stalls. We also learned to milk the cows. In the fall, we picked pears and apples. In payment, we were allowed to take some of them home. He sometimes gave us some milk or the rind from a slab of cheese. The rind looked like a long yellow snake, and Mutti said that it was very healthy. Sometimes he gave us some bread as well. A piece of the rind and a slice or two of bread made a good meal.

On one of the days, Mutti came home with some cream of wheat. She cooked it, let it dry, cut it in strips, and then fried it. It made a cozy meal.

Real sugar was hard to come by. For a treat when we had flour, Mutti made cookies sweetened with beets. We called them red beet cookies.

It wasn't that our neighbors had nothing. The war had not devastated this area. We found out that the mayors of the towns of Germany had been commanded to find housing for German refugees. The people obeyed, but resented the law and felt no responsibility or compassion for us.

I remembered when we had plenty and were always warm. That was in Poland in the three years before our escape.

20

Jutta

1942-1945

Wartegau, Poland

Schloss Parken

WE MOVED to Poland when I was six. Vati had gone to the war, and the bombs were falling in Berlin. One of Mutti's brothers, Onkel Biller, was given responsibility for us. He and his wife, Tante Britta, and another of Mutti's sisters, Tante Luci and her husband, Onkel Hans, as well as their mother, my Omi, were already living in Poland. Hitler had given my uncles large homes on great estates with Polish servants to help with everything.

We moved in with my Onkel Hans and Tante Luci. We were given two bedrooms on the second floor of their grand house. They were large, comfortable rooms with big beds, a rose-colored sofa, warm carpets, and a fireplace in each room. The servants made sure that there was plenty of wood, and they kept the fires burning when it was cold outside. Every evening, they would light the glass and metal oil lamps that sat on the tables which gave the rooms a warm glow.

We were scared of Onkel Hans. Whenever he went out or met with other men, he wore a dark uniform with a shiny buckle. He never smiled. We were not comfortable playing or being noisy when he was near, but he was away often.

We were not allowed to play with the Polish children who lived nearby because we were told they were subhuman. We would watch them sledding down a hill or sliding across the ice on special sleds on the lake behind the house. The ice sleds were only eighteen inches long. The children would kneel on them and push themselves along with a stick with a nail in its end. They could slide at a great speed.

Naturally, we cared more about having fun than we did about matters of politics.

On one of the days when we were watching from a window, Wasko, our Polish butler, showed us that we could sneak outside through a low window. After that, we spent fun afternoons playing with our new friends. We would have contests to see who could glide across the ice the fastest.

Our fun lasted until Onkel Hans found out. He was furious. He commanded that we never play with them again. We were not to have anything to do with sub-humans. We obeyed out of fear, not because we agreed with him, and not out of respect or love. Whatever we were forbidden to do, we wanted to do more.

Wasko was our ally at meals as well. He would serve the food wearing his black pants and white jacket with its two rows of gold buttons. Walter and I hated the soups made with pumpkin or mushrooms. Onkel Hans had a rule that we were to eat everything we were served. Wasko found ways to distract the adults or would watch until they weren't looking, and then would whisk our bowls away before we had finished.

Wasko showed us how to ride the dumbwaiter down to the kitchen. It was a little box of an elevator, just big enough for a few trays of food or for either Walter or me. One of us would climb in, Wasko would close the door, and then he would pull the ropes that would move the dumbwaiter down to the floor below where we would open the door and hop out.

The kitchen was always warm. The wood stove pumped out delicious smells of roasts or cakes in preparation for the coming meal. The cooks would sometimes let us sample a goody that was just coming out of the oven. The baker even taught me how to bake a little cake. We learned some Polish words from them, something we would not dare tell Mutti or any of the other adults.

When the weather was good, Wasko found time to teach me how to ride a bicycle. He would encourage me whenever I fell off.

Wasko also drove Walter and me to school. School was in a neighboring village, and it was too far away to walk. He would hitch a pony to a two-wheeled cart. We would sit behind him with a dust robe over our laps in the warm weather and a fur blanket when it was cold. Bells attached to the pony's harness would ring merrily as we rode along.

School was a frightening place. All of our teachers were German, as were all of our classmates. I don't know if the Polish children went to school, but if so, they were not allowed in ours. We learned songs that glorified Hitler and his rules. We were taught to read and write the old German alphabet and wrote with a quill dipped in ink. It wasn't easy.

If you forgot to greet your teacher with "Heil Hitler," you got your ear slapped or some other punishment. Once I was slapped across my face with the end of my braid. I got a black star next to my name that day. Girls who were not learning well were slapped across their open hand with a ruler. Once, Walter got his ear slapped so hard it hurt for days. We watched boys who were struggling with the lessons forced to kneel on hard, dried peas. Their uniforms were short pants in the summer – their knees had no protection.

Most of us had blond hair and blue eyes. We girls wore traditional German dresses or skirts with a traditional style of blouse. Most of us had long braids. You were considered to have a disease or to be a rebel if your hair was short.

Each morning started with raising the flag and singing the swastika song, "Die Fahne Hoch." For recess, we marched while we sang other songs that glorified Hitler or the German state. They were easy, catchy tunes that would stay in your mind. There were also sad songs about valiant soldiers who died in the war.

After school, Wasko would be waiting in the pony cart. The evenings were dinner and homework.

Sometimes Onkel Hans would have men over. They would sit in the salon, the house's fancy living room, and talk and smoke. One afternoon, Walter and I were watching through the keyhole. We heard Onkel Hans talking about his horses. One of the men asked him to bring his favorite horse there so that they could see it. He was joking, but the others took it up and bet that Onkel Hans would not do it. We ran away from the door when Onkel Hans came out. We hid to watch to see what would happen. A few minutes later, Hans came riding his white horse into the house across the marble floor of the entry hall and right into the salon. There was lots of laughter until the horse raised her tail and deposited on the pink Persian carpet what she had eaten a few hours ago! We ran back to our rooms so that he wouldn't hear us laugh.

A few times in the summers, Onkel Hans and Tante Luci would hold hunting parties. People in fancy clothes were dropped off at the entry, and their coachmen drove their carriages out to the stables. The servants treated them as very special guests, bowing to them and doing everything they asked. When they were starting the hunt, they would blow trumpets, and the dogs would bark. It was exciting to see them ride away.

There were parties at many meals and often a ball at the end of the day. Delicious meals were served. The rabbit and venison were the best.

We children had a great time. We either ate before the adults, or we sat at the far end of the table. One adult would be our supervisor. Somehow, we got away with hilarious food fights – throwing pickles at each other – with our cousins who were visiting from their estates nearby.

The food – potatoes, rabbit, bread, sausage, sauerkraut, and cakes with apples, gooseberries, and currants – was wonderful.

We were never hungry.

21
Jutta
Winter 1945-1946
Oberstaufen, Germany

The Eibelesmühle

I LONGED for the comfort of those times in Poland, but life at the Eibelesmühle wasn't all bad. There were times that winter when we went sledding with the neighbors' children. We piled into a long toboggan and went flying down a long slope near the pear trees. One of the fathers even made us some skis. They were made from the bent wood from the sides of barrels. Our boots were held on with ropes. They worked well and gave us the ability to ski into the village.

Walter and I played make-believe. He was the preacher or the father coming home from the war. He would deliver fiery sermons on how we would become better people if we obeyed authority. He was the authority!

There was a sawmill nearby. On a windy day, we took umbrellas and stood on a pile of wood with the umbrellas open. Walter gave the signal, and we would jump. He wanted the wind to carry us away to somewhere better. We always fell flat.

When Mutti had to go into the village, she would put me in charge. That is when the fights would start. Walter,

Elke, Heidi, and I quarreled over the one pencil we all wanted for coloring. Sharing was not easy when there was so little.

Christmas that year was sparse. We had one piece of bread to share among all of us. The night before St. Nicholas Day, Mutti still had us put out our shoes even though we did not expect to find any gifts in them the next day. Somehow, she had a rubber toy for each of us. They were little animals that had a hole and could squirt water. We had fun with them.

For a Christmas tree, we brought in a branch of an evergreen tree. Someone gave us some candles. We sang "Silent Night."

I couldn't help but remember the Christmases with Omi and our cousins in Poland.

22

Jutta

1942-1943

Wartegau, Poland

Christmas in Poland

CHRISTMAS WITH our cousins and Omi, our grandmother, were great occasions. Onkel Biller and Tante Britta and their five children lived just a few miles from where we lived with Onkel Hans and Tante Luci. When we visited, there were nine of us cousins and, on special occasions, our two cousins from Dresden came as well.

Omi would play with us. One of our favorites was "Come Home, My Sheep." Omi would sit on a big chair in the ballroom and call to us from across the room.

We would answer, "We can't come home."

She would say, "Why not?"

"We're afraid of the wolf. He could eat us."

"Come here. I'll protect you."

Then we would run as fast as we could to get to her before the wolf would come out of hiding, sometimes out of the grandfather clock, and catch us. If the wolf caught us, we had to sit with Omi and not play again. I was not the fastest runner and didn't like the roughness that accompanied the chases, but it was exciting.

Another game we loved was "Blind Cow." Omi would tie a scarf over the eyes of one of us. The blind one would need to catch us by feeling his way around the "pasture" while we taunted him but tried to run away before he caught us.

Another game also used a blindfold. Omi would put a piece of candy under an upside-down pot. The person who was "it" would be blindfolded and would be given a wooden spoon. He would crawl and hit the floor around him in order to find the pot by "feeling" with the spoon. The others were allowed to call out "warm" or "cold" to tell him if he was heading in the right direction. When he hit the pot, he would be rewarded with the candy. The cook made delicious caramel candies. They were a real prize.

Omi even let us play hide and seek, a game that was forbidden by the other adults.

When we needed a special treat, she would take us down to the kitchen and make us goggel moggel. It was a frothy dessert made of egg yolks flavored with sugar or chocolate.

She would tell us stories about when she was a girl, and she would sing sad songs. There was one in particular, "Ich hatt' einen Kamaraden," that she loved. It was about a young soldier dying in the war. I think it reminded her of Jürgen, one of her sons who had died fighting the Russians.

We didn't see our cousins only at Christmas. Their manor was close enough that we could take a short train ride or come by carriage. Arriving at their house was special. There was a wide area in front where the carriage would drop us off. After we got out, the coachman would guide the horses to the stable. At night there were lanterns with candles inside the carriage and two outside lighting the way.

Mutti loved being near her mother and the family. The men were often away, but Omi and my Tante Britta and the servants took good care of us.

23

Jutta

Spring 1946

Rheden, Germany

Family

I KNEW Mutti missed Omi and the rest of the family. She knew they had escaped from Poland, but she didn't know how to get in touch with them. That spring, Mutti was able to contact them. Omi, Onkel Biller, Tante Britta, and our cousins were living in the town of Rheden, south of the city of Hannover in northern Germany. Mutti decided that we should leave the Eibelesmühle and join them. They had welcomed us in Poland. They would welcome us now.

When we arrived in Rheden, we found our relatives in a castle that they were sharing with the owners. It was a wonderful reunion. We made a large, noisy family. We did not talk much about what had happened in the past year, although I did learn that Omi and the family had moved from Poland in a covered wagon lined with their Persian rugs. They brought a few of our things as well. The trunk with feather comforters and the warm clothes were wonderful. I wished we had had them in the winter.

Tante Britta was always gentle and kind. She allowed me to work with her in her garden picking tomatoes, strawberries, chives, and potatoes. I have always enjoyed helping people.

Tante Britta taught us how to make a ball with pieces of cloth. We had fun using it for all sorts of games. A rope that we found in the stable made a good jump rope. We collected pieces of porcelain and used the flat bits to play hopscotch. We found ways to have fun without spending money.

We saw many refugees walking the roads with all of their possessions in knapsacks on their backs. I wondered where they would find homes. We knew that we were fortunate to have found our relatives.

But it didn't last. With the addition of my brother and sisters, there were nine of us children. The owners were required by the law to take in refugees, but two families were too much even for their castle. Onkel Biller worked with the authorities and found us another host in a town a few miles west of there.

It had been only a month, but we had to move again.

24
Tom
Winter-Summer 1945
Budapest
Oros, Hungary

Liberation

THE CHANGE that had taken place in my heart when I took Jesus as my Messiah was evident soon thereafter. As I went near one of the windows facing the street, I noticed a German soldier half a block away holding his machine gun and occasionally firing between two small shrubs. Instead of wanting to kill him like I had before, I felt a touch of pity. I realized that he was an unfortunate, misled person who was on the wrong track of life. I also saw that he was being used as human ammunition for his higher-ups as they pursued their insane and evil goal. Would he realize his folly if he knew God? It was barely two minutes later that his body keeled over and the helmet rolled off his head.

Our physical, military liberation from the Nazis was totally anticlimactic. One night we began hearing warnings in Hungarian over giant loudspeakers. "Soviet forces have surrounded Budapest. Any resistance will lead only to a futile extension of bloodshed." After waiting for so long for the possibility of survival, Soviets were within a few hundred yards.

Airplanes roared overhead spraying the streets with lethal machine gun fire. Shelling became so violent that we dared only leave the basement for minutes a day to accomplish essential tasks. Fetching cold water from the nearby well became hazardous.

One morning, a shabbily clad fellow with a strange fur hat appeared at the door of our basement shelter just as I had stepped outside to breathe a bit of fresh air. To my shock and delight I noticed on his hat the enameled red star with the hammer and sickle. He wandered in calmly and casually, carrying an automatic rifle as he looked around for hiding German and Hungarian Nazis.

I greeted him with joy and fear. He asked only one question:

"Any Germans?"

"No," I said. "Only Jews!"

He made no comment, just looked around once again and left the place. I stared at his back in a daze.

I ran to the others in the basement and yelled, "The Russians are here!"

There was no jubilation. We were too skeptical to believe good news. What will the rest of them be like? What if a German counterattack recaptures our area?

This scene repeated itself a few more times during the day. Airplane attacks quickly gave way to the installation of grenade launchers in our backyard by busy crews wearing fur hats with the red star. The five launchers were loaded with one grenade after another and the windows rattled with each explosion.

I clearly recall thinking to myself at the time that if I ever have a small room with a window through which some sunshine or daylight can come in, some bread and water, and security from bombings and persecution, if then I cannot be content, I will know that I have lost my perspective.

Fortunately, this thought has followed me to this day, helping me to be thankful in circumstances marred by "problems" which in comparison qualify as nothing more than minor inconveniences.

There was a life to be restarted, and we did not waste much time. With Russian soldiers everywhere, we did not dare to be on the streets after dusk, but during the day, we did get around in the neighborhood. The stores were closed, but adventurous grocers, farmers, and bakers crawled out of their hiding places, and businesses started to become alive again as the Russian artillery moved westward. Money was scarce, and trading became the name of the game. The main boulevards became endless flea markets where people sold whatever they had and bought or traded for whatever they needed most.

Our priorities were to find my Bözsike Néni and to decide where to live. Our first journey took us to the ghetto where we were delighted to find Bözsike Néni alive and well. We also found Béla Bácsi and Rózus Néni, my uncle and aunt who had also survived in the Budapest Ghetto.

With some excitement, we set out with Bözsike to see if our home had survived the battle. The chances of finding everything intact were minimal. Whatever we had left there would have become the possession of the Hungarian Nazi tenants who took it over after we were displaced. They would have escaped once the Russians came in, fearing a confrontation with us. What they had left was up for grabs for looters who swarmed around the rubble. We walked along the war-torn streets with anticipation, but seeing the results of shelling and bombing everywhere, we prepared ourselves to find the place in ruins.

As we turned the corner onto our street to catch a first glimpse of the familiar apartment house, our eyes widened, and we stopped to take in the scene. The only thing left standing was the frame of the building without windows or front wall and with most of the floors sagging between the main supports.

Toward the end of the war, the high school across the street had been secretly converted into an ammunition depot. A few days after we had intended to hide there on our way to the "orphanage," well-placed Allied bombs had hit the depot resulting in an explosion of many tons of ammunition demolishing the entire surrounding block.

As we walked toward the rubble that was our former home, I looked up to the sunny sky to thank God that we had been spared. To our delight, we found the drawers containing our photo albums which had somehow been protected from damage during weeks of exposure to the elements. Picking up these and a few other souvenirs, we glanced at the remains of our large steel-framed aquarium and realized silently that we had lost nearly everything. As dear as these things were to us, we felt only limited pain at their loss. Relief at being alive and our gratefulness to God for having spared us helped us through the experience of loss.

I am most grateful that my parents spent their discretionary funds primarily on family experiences, travel, and fun with friends, as well as on helping those who had less than we had. This allowed me to walk away rich with the memories of happy times while we lived in that place.

The main cause for sorrow was the news of loved ones no longer expected to return from prisoner-of-war (POW) camps or from the death camps. We anxiously awaited news about my father once the lines of communication were gradually restored.

We found an abandoned apartment on the second floor of a building within a few blocks of our destroyed home. Mother made arrangements for us to occupy it until we would know more about our future. We then went back to the "orphanage" to bid farewell to the others and to collect our few belongings, including the new Bibles we had been given by Mary and Emil.

Food

We began to settle into our new life. The important commodities were flour, bacon, sugar, honey, and coffee, closely followed by dried or canned vegetables and preserves. The currency was beginning to show signs of weakness, and gold, silver, and jewelry became the reference values. I remember when Mother traded her gold Swiss Doxa watch for ten pounds of flour. We had a fried dough splurge that night and cherished every bite.

Within a week or two, Budapest became a beehive of activity. The sun was shining, and, while we were poor, we felt rich.

We were FREE!

News About Father

The nagging question on our minds was, "What happened to Father?"

While we were grateful to God that he was sent to the Russian front and not to the death camps, we wondered whether we would ever see him again.

Those of us who had relatives who had "disappeared" on the Russian front watched lists of names, updated daily, of those who trickled back from POW camps. Mother and I had a strange assurance that God would lead Father home safely. We were sure that a family with such a strong bond of love would be reunited.

One day, the doorbell of our apartment rang, but no one stood at the door. We went to the rear balcony corridor and looked down to the street. We recognized the man with whom my father had shared what we had sent him. This was the soft-spoken, kind, circus weightlifter whose company I had enjoyed when Mother and I had the chance to visit my father.

"Is Miklós alive?" my mother shouted.

"Yes!" he answered.

Our heartbeats accelerated as we ran down the stairs to meet him. Obviously, he would bring word from my father. His cheerful smile assured us that he had good news. I beat Mother to embrace the man. "How is my father? Where is he? When can we see him?"

We bombarded him with questions without giving him the chance to even say hello. Once we calmed down, he put his hand on my shoulder, shook my mother's hand warmly, and told us that Father was well, but far away. He had contracted some illness, a result of malnutrition and the stress of the past years. He himself had walked for days from the POW camp to board a freight train, and then endured weeks of innumerable transfers and delays before finally arriving in Budapest.

He told us that if my mother wanted to talk to my father on the phone, he could arrange it from one of the Russian command posts in a suburb of the city.

Mother was ecstatic to go right away, and so was I. However, he said he could not take children to the post, a rule apparently strictly enforced by the Russians.

Mother suggested that she would drop me off at a friend's place, and at the same time, ask Mr. Brichta, a friend of my father, if he would accompany her to the command post. My father could give his friend instructions for picking up the pieces of his business.

The man's response was, "Why don't you do that while I take care of an errand. I'll return to pick you up."

He never returned.

The next time we heard of him, his picture was on the front page of the newspapers. He was guilty of twelve rape-murders committed against the wives of his POW comrades using the same story he had tried on us. What saved my mother *(God's saving hand!)* was her insistence on bringing along Mr. Brichta, my father's friend.

It was only on death row, a few days before he was hanged, that the man was ready to talk to Mother and tell her the truth.

Father had fallen into Russian captivity – ironically, a Jew's only hope for survival – and contracted typhoid fever. He passed away in 1943, his war and sickness-tormented body finding rest in an unmarked grave in a foreign land.

Mother did not share this news with me, but she had tears in her eyes when she walked through the door one day. Without speaking, she went directly to her bedroom. It was apparent that she did not wish to talk about a matter which bothered her. I was not about to ask but wondered what it could have been.

Within a few days, I received an invitation to have dinner with our Bible study leader. I was delighted but thought it strange that Mother would not be going too. On the night that I was to go, I lay down for a brief rest before going out. Wondering what the two of us would talk about, I had a sudden realization. "He is going to tell me that my father is dead." It dawned on me that Mother, unable to bring herself to tell me the news, had sought outside assistance.

I was sobbing uncontrollably when Mother entered the room. Bewildered, she approached me and asked, "What's wrong?"

I looked at her and replied, "I know that Father is dead! There is no need to have someone else tell me."

Mother sat down next to me and reached out her hand to comfort me. I continued to sob as she told me the crushing truth.

Farm

Mary Hajos was continuing her God-given mission of caring for others, including us. She saw that we could use a place where we could rest and have better food than was available in the war-torn city. She contacted a farmer who was willing to take in Mother, Bözsike Néni, and me for some compensation, which included my willingness to serve as a farm hand. Mother sold her last pieces of jewelry in exchange for some cash, and we left for four months in the country. The farm was located in the village of Oros, about ten miles from Nyiregyhaza, my father's birthplace.

In addition to looking forward to more and healthier food and lots of fresh air, I liked the idea of adding farm life to my city background. The likelihood of school starting up again was remote, so we took the opportunity with anticipation.

Train Trip

We packed a few necessities and set out on the 120-mile journey. There were no scheduled trains and no passenger cars left in the country. They had been used in the last days of the Nazi regime for one-way westward trips primarily for those who wanted to avoid potential prosecution by the Hungarian judicial system after the war would be over.

Some people had a good feel for when freight trains were to depart and were able to find a place for themselves inside a freight car. Those of us who arrived a little late had to be satisfied with a place on top. My mother, Bözsike Néni, and I spread a blanket on top of a car and prepared to stay, if necessary, for days.

It was a free ride, but a rugged one. The railway signal system was not operating, and most of the locomotives had also gone westward with the passenger cars. The few trains that were running moved slowly to eliminate a potential crash in the sight-based "control system."

We learned to sleep under the sky on top of the moving car without rails to protect us from rolling down. The idea was to lie at least two yards away from the edge, tying ourselves to each other, and taking turns staying awake and watching for trouble. We ate more and more sparingly as the journey became prolonged. We took our chances with our toileting needs, climbing down the ladder at the end of the car during the frequent, unscheduled stops, with one eye on the train in case it began to move.

It took us two days to travel the 120 miles. It was a relief to see a large sign for the city of Nyiregyhaza appear at the side of the railroad station in the distance. The train came to a halt, and we returned to terra firma. We found our host, who was holding a sign with our name on it. He welcomed us graciously and helped us board his horse-driven carriage. We let Bözsike Néni sit next to him on the padded driver's seat while Mother and I made ourselves as comfortable as we could among our pieces of luggage.

On the Farm

I have never regretted the opportunity to learn about life on a farm. I had not realized the tremendous and steady physical demands that it required in this period before extensive mechanization.

At times the weather was too hot to work during the day. On these occasions, the farmer, his daughter, and I would go out in the cool of the evening to collect and stack hay eight feet high on the wagon. This was followed by a ride home under the stars.

I learned to ride horses, drive a carriage, care for farm animals, and whistle – with four fingers in my mouth – loudly enough to be heard from a distance. I became good at cracking a whip and making it sound like a gunshot, and at doing various jobs on the farm and around the house.

Bible Readings and Church

Following my spiritual rebirth, I could not contain the news about what I had found. I asked permission to lead Bible readings after the evening meal. These sessions brought us together as if we were part of their family. We also went to church together on Sundays and got to know and enjoy time with the local parishioners.

Taming Micza

I even attempted to ride Micza, a beautiful one-year-old horse nobody had attempted to tame. The farmer warned me not to even think of a venture with her, which, of course, made it an enticing challenge.

I chose a careful approach. I gave Micza a nice portion of corn with her meal twice a day and made sure she saw who the donor was. The following week, I took her to the well on the hotter days, instead of just letting her drink from the trough in the stall. Once I assumed Micza and I had a friendship, after each feeding I placed the saddle on her back and mounted her while she was still bound to her post.

No problem.

One sunny Sunday afternoon, dressed in nice pants and an open white shirt, I was ready for the test. The village was quiet after Sunday lunch, so I did not have to fear public ridicule. I mounted Micza, untied the rope from her post, and gently nudged her towards the stall door. She calmly obeyed. I wished all our neighbors were there now watching my success. Once out in the open, Micza, who apparently was thirsty, glanced at the well, and suddenly I found myself flat on the ground. She had thrown me off, kicked backwards, and left a horseshoe-shaped print on my shirt. It was a close call and the end of my career as a horseback rider.

The farmer smiled when I reported the event. "Thomas, you are fortunate you got away without more damage."

School and the Bull

A few months into our time at the farm, my mother thought she should check whether school was in session. To our surprise, my friends were all back in school. We learned that unless I caught up to where they were in the curriculum, I would be held back. Determined to not be left behind, I began tutoring with a young graduate of the high school in Nyiregyhaza who lived across town.

The twenty-minute, late afternoon walk to and from her place was a healthy break from studying intensively all day. My walk often coincided with a herd of cows returning from the field. The cowherds assured me on several occasions that the cows posed no danger to me walking home.

However, one day I noticed that one of the bulls had pulled out in front of the herd, his chain loosely dangling from his neck, and not a cowherd in sight. I could see the wrinkles in the bull's neck, with only fifty feet between us. I was terrified.

He charged. I jumped over a low fence and hid behind a storage shack. The bull wandered around a bit, then continued down the street. Clearly, I was not cut out to play torero, and let out a sigh of relief as I continued my journey towards home.

My intensive studies paid off when a few weeks later I successfully passed the examination that would allow me to join my classmates at the start of the new school year. The report card I received while studying with my tutor was the only one on which I ever received a perfect score for conduct!

Refreshed physically and mentally, we were ready to restart our life in the city. This time we rode in style, with seats in a restored passenger car, and completed the journey in less than four hours.

25

Tom

1946-1950

Budapest

New Era

IT WAS quite an eye-opener for us to see how much life had stabilized since we had left for the country. While collapsed bridges, ruined and bullet-ridden buildings, and other signs of the war were visible everywhere, life had returned to normal. Restaurants, theaters, and soccer stadiums were full of people ready to build a new future. Schools resumed their activities, and we became part of the upswing.

Mother and Bözsike Néni got the dressmaking business going, picking up the pieces of their father's business. I rejoined my secondary school, which had dismissed the teachers who had fallen for the Nazi ideology.

Mother and I joined a weekly Bible study arranged by a Messianic Jewish Bible teacher mainly for new Jewish believers who needed some time to feel comfortable among Gentile believers. We also began attending a Calvinist church. Although we enjoyed the sermons, somehow we never developed close relationships with the others gathered there. The gap between Jews and Gentiles could not get completely erased even among believers.

Influential Movies

At the age of fourteen, I saw a movie on the life of the great American engineer-inventor Thomas Edison. His creativity and perseverance made a formidable impression on me. After learning about him, I never considered any career other than engineering.

I was longing to harness my modest talents to serve others with the spirit I observed in a movie on the life of a giant in another field, Hungarian doctor Ignác Semmelweis. He had invested his life in researching maternal mortality and discovered the importance of handwashing and the use of antiseptic techniques during childbirth.

These two movies directed my mind toward finding a profession that would be stimulating, in line with my innate abilities, and beneficial to people.

As a result of the impression that these documentaries left on me, I strongly believe in youth finding something that fascinates them and suits their unique talents. This often results in progress toward making life better.

Boy Scouts

Having lost my father and being an only child, I responded quickly to my friend Andy's suggestion that I check out the Jewish Boy Scout "Toldi" troop he so enjoyed.

As we descended the stairs into the air raid shelter on Sallai Imre Street, the noise of a lively bunch of boys sounded inviting. Andy introduced me to one of the senior Boy Scouts who asked a few questions, stretched out his hand, and welcomed me into the troop.

No fancy equipment was needed. We had good leadership, some sturdy tables with long benches, a few bare light bulbs, and a ping pong table. Yet the place was like a beehive almost every evening as the various patrol groups held their weekly meetings.

Hikes every weekend, overnight camping several times a year, and a two-week summer camp filled us with excitement. Our motivation to participate in the weekly hikes was enhanced by the rule that if we missed more than three in a given year, we were not allowed to stay in the troop.

We had competitions and games with other patrols. My favorite was the number war game. We would each have a blue or pink paper with a large black number strapped to our head with a rubber band. The goal was to keep the enemy from seeing the number, calling it out, and thus "killing" you. The team with the most players at the end was the winner. I was especially good at it and was given free reign by my patrol mates to find and shout out the numbers of our enemies, instead of being asked to be part of a group.

We learned how to use things we found in the wild to create what we had not brought along, or we learned how to manage with the bare necessities. We realized how little we actually needed of the supplies and equipment we had thought were essential. We learned how to share the little we had, and to cooperate and coexist even when we were cold, sleep deprived, or when a strenuous hike had put our patience and reasoning to the test.

I shared my faith with my patrol mates who, to my surprise, became interested, and our leader asked me if I could get an introductory Bible class going. A Christian minister of Jewish descent gladly obliged and led our discussions for several months. Eventually, however, attendance fell off, we stopped meeting, and the subject was tabled.

My favorite reading was the Boy Scout equipment catalog, occasionally obtained from America. We envied those guys, who had their choice of all those wonderful gadgets. We imagined American cities and towns swarming with Boy Scouts out on their weekly excursions.

Of some concern to Mother was the fact that being a Boy Scout became my primary commitment while my high school studies and projects were completed in my "spare time."

I think back to the Boy Scout years as one of the best and most useful periods of my life. I am particularly grateful to our patrol leader, who taught us to go on when we thought we were at the very end of our rope. He helped us learn to carry out the mission regardless of a change in circumstances. This mentality to persevere and the "rain or shine" approach frequently saved us from the dilemma of indecision and freed us from thinking about too many alternatives and options.

Joining this troop turned out to be one of the most significant and rewarding decisions of my life, one that continues to affect me to this day. I became part of a wonderful group of boys led by superb leaders who provided me with an incredible combination of fun, training, and character-shaping discipline so crucial in a teenager's life.

Friendships developed in those years became life-long bonds despite living in countries scattered around the globe. We continue to gather on a regular basis both in the countries we live in and in Hungary every two to three years. Our children and even grandchildren have joined us, making friends with one another and witnessing and absorbing some of the "Toldi Spirit."

In 1948, three years after I joined the Boy Scouts, the Communists, having taken over the government in the three years since the end of the war, aborted the Boy Scout movement. I became somewhat of a loner but, ironically, did not feel lonely. I did not feel accepted in Christian circles, which was not necessarily their fault. I lost contact with most of my former friends and did not develop new close friendships.

High School

In our school system, we had four years of elementary school followed by eight years of "gymnasium" which was a combination of junior and senior high schools. Our gymnasium years were drab. The Communist regime had no interest in adding uplifting events to our school years.

We were expected to take part in the Communist youth group called Pioneers. There was no comparison to the Boy Scouts. The main activities were political rallies. I took part in the rallies and for a while was taken in by the Communist ideals. I read a book about life lived together for the common good that touched me to tears. It seemed like a dream. I fell into the trap that this was a good thing for the country and that they were doing for the poor what Jesus taught.

I had given up reading my Bible on a regular basis. Because of the pressure of the Communist teaching, attending church and particularly home Bible studies became increasingly difficult for one who worked or planned to enter college or university.

I pursued hobbies such as indoor gardening, taking care of the tropical fish in my tank, soccer, tennis, and occasional skiing. I enjoyed attending concerts and listening to classical music.

To this day, I find it hard to understand how I settled for just hanging in. I did not feel like a loser, but neither did I feel like any kind of a winner. I lived in timeless time waiting for special events to surface or for something to rock my boat.

World Youth Conference

In 1948, the new government organized the World Youth Conference and Festival. The purpose was to invite youth from around the world to the beautiful city of Budapest and have them witness the amazing results of Communism. The Party hoped the visitors would be so impressed that they would agitate for Communism in their home countries.

Conditions had been on the upswing, and it seemed as if everyone was happy. Shops were full of merchandise, and the streets were filled with satisfied faces. Music and dancing filled the air. Our visitors, however, were unaware that behind the lively performances, our lives were actually quite drab. Also, the ticket prices for visitors were very low or sometimes even free, but for a local like me, they were prohibitive.

One evening, I was interested in a performance of Hungarian music and dance. I was watching the crowd as they entered the National Theater, wondering how I might get in.

I heard a group of young people speaking English.

I approached them, "Do you mind if I join you? I'm Hungarian, but I speak English. I want to pretend I'm part of your group."

They were happy to embrace me as one of their own. I smiled and waved to the theater staff at the door as I entered with the group. They had a row of seats reserved – good seats! Shortly after the show started, a Hungarian lady sitting behind me leaned forward and asked with a big smile if I would like her to sing softly in my ear the songs she knew. Each time she began singing, I thanked her graciously in broken Hungarian, followed by, "Thank you, Madam. Thank you." I kept rewarding her with grateful smiles and silent claps. I even autographed her ticket, using "Tom Howard" as an alias, for her to keep as a souvenir. Following the performance, I introduced her to my English "compatriots," a treat she seemed to cherish.

Outside the theater, we were surrounded by Hungarian youth sticking small notepads and pens toward us to get the autographs of their English guests. Under the streetlights, I took a small risk by signing "William Shakespeare" about twenty times, receiving thanks every time. I imagined them bragging about their "catch" the next day and their reactions when their parents and teachers would tell them that they had likely been taken.

On one of the festival days, a policeman caught me jaywalking. "I am sorry. I am sorry," I said in English. Embarrassed, he apologized, took my arm and led me across the street with a smile. We parted as friends. He must have felt good about having shown kindness to a visitor to Hungary!

After the Youth Festival, it occurred to me that something was wrong. Suddenly, everything stopped appearing in the shop windows. It became completely clear to me that this was a lousy regime, and I should have nothing to do with supporting it in the future.

Exam

The climax of gymnasium was the "Senior Matriculation," an excruciating test at the end of the senior year. We had to pass written and oral tests in six subjects within a two-week period covering all the material from the past eight years.

We had two months of study time to prepare for this test. All of us sat at our desks at home or in the library for eight to ten hours a day. We looked at every adult who appeared to have passed this test in his or her younger years with great envy. It was not uncommon for students who were unable to cope with the strain to break down, in some cases committing suicide. The test was a cruel exercise, but I felt God's powerful presence through it all. I needed top results badly because my political record was poor, due to having attended church and Bible study regularly and the fact that my father had been a capitalist, evident because he had been in business.

There were no year-end celebrations or graduation ceremonies. We were handed our high school diplomas on the last day of our final tests without even a word of congratulations or good wishes. All the regime cared about was duty, loyalty, and getting through the task of education.

26

Jutta

1946-1950

Marienhagen, Germany

Rebuilding

WHEN WE left Onkel Biller and Tante Tutti and the castle, we moved a few miles west to Marienhagen. It was a peaceful village in the middle of rolling farmland. The Hartz mountains in the distance were a nice backdrop to the green fields. It was refreshing to see houses that had not been destroyed by the war. For some reason, the armies left this area alone. But life was no easier than in other areas of the country. The economy of the whole nation was gone.

We were given two rooms in a house belonging to Frau Fischer. Her husband must have been lost in the war because we never saw him. She hated us from the start, but she was required to take us in. We four slept in one room and the other became our living room and kitchen. It had a small black wood stove that provided warmth and served as our cook stove.

There was never enough food, but finally we were not afraid of starving. The British were in control of our area of Germany, and the ration cards they gave out once a month made sure we had something. You had to plan your meals according to the ration cards so that you didn't run out before the end of the month. When we got cards for cigarettes, we traded them with someone else for food items.

Butter, cans of tuna fish, and cheese were some of what we could get with the ration cards. There was gooey, bright yellow cheese that came in buckets. We would eat it with a spoon. It was strange, but wonderful. Then there was yellow bread. We had never seen cornmeal before. When I was given our first loaf, I ran home asking Mutti why the bread was yellow. What had they put in it?

When the Germans were asked what we needed most, the answer was "Korn." This is the German word for grain. The Americans heard "corn" and assumed we wanted cornbread. It filled us up, but it was not the bread we were expecting.

We stood in line for everything. Once Mutti sent me to a neighboring village with a jar with a metal lid to be filled with some cottage cheese. There were at least twenty people already in line, but I went home with a full jar. At other times, I stood in lines for cabbage, bread, sugar, butter, and milk. Sometimes the butter was rancid, but we ate it anyway.

When we were able to get good butter and some sugar, Mutti would make us schmand bon bons. It was a delicious candy similar to fudge.

Some nights, Walter and I stole carrots from a neighboring farm. The farmer must have understood because we didn't get in trouble.

There were CARE packages from the United States as well. *(I have learned since that these were from the organization called the Cooperative for American Remittances to Europe.)* They were distributed by the mayor's people or by one of the soldiers. They had cheese, milk powder, canned meat, rice, flour, sugar, chocolate, butter, and other food. Some also contained toys, paper and pencils, and other nice things. We had never seen crayons before they arrived in a package. It was thrilling to discover that you could write and draw with them. There were coloring books as well. *(Coloring books still hold a warm spot in my heart.)* Another package had towels. How did they know that we needed them?

One of the packages included a beautiful dress. It was pleated and had pink and light blue stripes on a dark blue background. A mother must have packed that box. I loved the dress so much I didn't want to take it off at night. I felt so special. Another package had a pair of gold shoes. We girls fought over them. "You've had them for an hour. It's my turn."

We were given some rabbits. As cute and cuddly as they were, they also were delicious. I had the job of killing and skinning them. At first, it was hard to hold one and slit its throat, but hunger is a strong force. We also were given some chickens. Plucking them was a messy job, but it was worth the effort. I learned how to skin a deer. I didn't hunt them, but I was allowed to skin them and take some of the meat.

Mutti and I went out when it was dark to pick some apples from the ground. Suddenly the farmer was there with his two German shepherd dogs barking loudly. He told us to drop the apples we had collected.

We rode our bicycles to a nearby town where we could pick blueberries. I found that it was most encouraging to fill a small cup and see that my picking had amounted to something before pouring the berries into the big bucket.

There were nuts to be gathered in the woods. We would tie bags to our ankles and fill them with the nuts. Because they were wild and did not belong to anyone, we could sell them at the market or trade them for other things.

Mutti would often get called away by Dr. Schmitz to help with the delivery of a baby or some other medical work. The doctor would come on his motorcycle, and Mutti would follow on her bicycle. Sometimes she would get food as payment for her work.

Once, a soldier stopped his Jeep and hopped out. He came over to me and picked me up. I saw that he was crying. He asked me in broken German if I had brothers and sisters. I said yes. He gave me a Hershey chocolate bar and told me to share it with them, but after he drove away, I hid behind some bushes and ate the whole thing by myself. It tasted so good!

The mayor allotted a little garden plot to us. We planted tomatoes, strawberries, string beans, and potatoes. It was my job to bring water in a bucket to water the plants.

Our hostess, Frau Fischer, resented having to take us in. She particularly hated Mutti. There was a day when we heard Mutti screaming. Walter and I ran out to the porch to find that Frau Fischer was holding a broom handle across Mutti's neck, had forced her to the railing and was pushing her over toward the pavement below. If we had not caught her feet and pulled her to safety she would have fallen and been badly hurt or would have died.

It was after that, that we found our chickens squashed to death. Another time, our bunnies were killed. We didn't see her do it, but we blamed Frau Fischer.

There was another family living in the house as well. The daughters of the family were older than I. They did all sorts of wonderful crafts. They made wall hangings, children's toys, and ornaments out of wood. They mostly sold them, but they occasionally gave us something they had made. They taught me how to make straw star ornaments. I would collect straw from the farms and cut the straws into exact lengths. I would fill the iron with hot coals from the stove and iron the straws flat. Then I would bind them together with thread.

My friends and I learned to make dolls out of pieces of material. Some of our dolls were flat with no belly or legs, made mostly of strips of fabric. Sometimes we were able to stuff them with old, soft underwear. Our imaginations added what they didn't have.

I still had Tipsi. I was fourteen years old when I stopped playing with her and the other dolls. Some of the other children teased me for still enjoying them at my old age!

We went to school there. It was the first time I had been settled in a school since we lived in Poland. I was in elementary school in the first three years. The school was in our village.

We had a lot of fun with pranks on our teachers. Someone put a piece of stinky cheese behind the radiator. The lesson stopped until the teacher cleaned it out. It took a while before our classroom smelled right again. There often were spitballs sailing around. The boys would bring straws, wad up bits of paper, put them in their mouths to make them round and hard, and then blow them out of the straw across the room. We girls were the targets at times. Sometimes someone was brave enough to aim at a teacher. There was the pig's tail that someone pinned to the skirt of one of the teachers when she was writing on the blackboard. She didn't discover it until someone pointed it out in the teachers' room. We had a good laugh. The teacher had a stick that she used for punishment. One of the boys said that if you rub the stick with an onion, it would become brittle and break. We discovered it was true! If anyone was caught, he had to write "A good conscience is a soft pillow" over and over.

In the first years after the war, we didn't have paper for our lessons. We had to cut the margins off newspapers and magazines and glue them together. When we didn't have glue, we had to write our stories in the margins.

I was not good with studying, but always worked hard. During a math test, I saw a squirrel outside and wished I were him because he didn't have to take the test. I preferred to help people, play with dolls, sew, or do crafts. I was especially bad with math. One of Mutti's friends would tutor me when the lesson was especially difficult. The math teacher was nice, but that didn't help me learn.

When I was finishing elementary school, Mutti wanted Walter and me to have a better education than what we could get in our own village. She enrolled us in a Gymnasium, a middle school that emphasized academics.

We had to walk or bike seven kilometers to the next village to get to the school. If we saw a dead animal on the way home, we would have a burial for it. We would put a sign on a stick, "Here rests a little bird" (or bunny or other animal). Sometimes, a kindly farmer would give us a ride on his tractor, or we would hop onto a wagon that was bringing chalk from the mines to the city. The wagons ran slowly along narrow rails. The conductor would call out, "Children, jump on!" We would sit on top of the chalk blocks in the container.

I made some friends. We would sew dolls, do crafts, play hopscotch, or other fun things. One of the friends was from Britain. She invited me to her house for tea. They served plum cake. It tasted good, but the family was stiff and formal. I was very glad when I could leave. I did not get a good impression of the British from that experience.

In the winters, we would go sledding down the main street. We would go out after dinner and sled until bedtime. We had been given flashlights that were powered by a crank on the side. The sound of the buzzing of the cranks was a part of those nights.

It was not all harmony at home. My brother and I used pens made from feathers that you had to dip in the ink, but we had only one inkpot.

I said, "Could you please give me the ink pot?"

"Don't you see that I need it right now?" Walter answered.

"But, I need it too!" I picked up a ruler. "If you don't give me the ink pot now I will whack you." The ink pot went flying. I cried, but Walter helped me clean it up.

The bakery sold more than bread. There was a table that had a basket with cheap jewelry and other things. I saw a pair of hair clips that were little boxes that would close over the end of a braid and lock it in place. They were red with little white daisies painted on top. I just HAD to have them. My hand jumped out and grabbed them.

I felt so horrible that as I walked home holding the hair clips, I was shivering with every step.

When I got there, Mutti asked, "Where did you get those things?"

My tears came.

Mutti said, "Turn right around. You go back."

I went through the village by myself. I told the baker, "I'm so sorry," and I burst into tears.

But the baker's wife who was standing nearby said, "Jutta, what is wrong?"

I said, "I have stolen these two hair clips."

Then she said I could keep them. I was so happy they were really mine, and I was relieved of the horrible guilt feeling.

When I was thirteen, the town had a Sportfeste. They had competitions in long jumping, foot races, and other track and field events. I came in first in the 500-meter race, even beating the boys. The prize was a laurel berry crown. I was on a podium when they gave it to me. People clapped and shouted, "Fantastic, Jutta. You did it!"

Walter said, "You always show off what a good runner you are. You always win. You run faster than me, but what you can't do is math!"

There was a big pillar where news was posted in the middle of the village. There were pictures hanging on it of men who had been in the war and were looking for their families. The American and British soldiers were working hard to reunite families.

One day, I was standing in line waiting for bread. A boy, the son of the postman, rode up to me on his bike. He said that they had found my father and that I should go home and tell my mother. I thought he was teasing since that was often my experience with boys. But after a few minutes of him trying to convince me, I decided to leave my place in line and go tell Mutti.

It was true! Mutti found out that Vati was in a camp in the south of Germany. The mayor told Mutti to go to the camp to find him.

It had been six years. I was six when he left, and now I was twelve. The four of us children lined up to greet him.

Heidi started to cry. She had been inside Mutti's womb when Vati was sent away. She was six now. She said, "I can't say 'father' to you. You are a stranger to me."

We each had our unique greeting. Walter said, "Vati, I flunked math."

I said, "Vati, I'm so glad you are back from the war because there is a big boy at school named William who is always teasing me. Now that you are home, you can protect me!"

Vati just stood there. He was probably wondering where to begin.

Vati knew that the war in Germany had been horrible. He was happy we were alive, even though we had nothing. At one time, he said, "You have to be patient with me. Six years I wasn't here. I have to readjust to your life."

Frau Fischer had to give us another room. Walter and I moved into a room in the attic. That left Mutti and Vati in the room that doubled as our kitchen and sitting room. Heidi and Elke had the room next to it.

Vati took over some of the tasks. He now did my job of drawing water and carrying the pails with a yoke over his shoulders. He built a ladder for the chickens to get in and out of their coop. Walter was happy to give him his job of splitting wood. He helped me with handwriting and math, two of the challenging subjects at school.

Vati was very handy. He cut up the leather suitcase that he had brought home and made each of us a pair of sandals. Before that, Mutti and I had been sharing one pair of shoes. Only one of us could go out at a time. Our sandals made us the envy of the other kids who didn't have new shoes. He had learned to make fuel that would be cheaper than logs for the stove. He would go to the sawmill and get sawdust. Then he had a way of packing the sawdust into bricks. They would burn in our stove for twenty-four hours.

Vati applied to the governing allies for a job. Before he was considered, they had to check his background to see whether he had committed any war crimes. They realized that he had not been in Europe during most of the war, and before that, he had been a weapons specialist teaching in the military academy. He also had never joined the Nazi party. The allies decided that he was not guilty.

Later in his life, we heard that when he was in the military before being sent to Japan, his unit was in a convoy moving through Poland. He saw Jewish people begging for food. At the rear of the convoy, trucks loaded with fish were headed for disbursement among the German troops. Vati loosened the ties of the rear gate of his truck and, when the convoy started up, a few barrels rolled off before others saw and tightened the gate again. He was glad to see the people dividing the fish between themselves as they drove away.

Once the allies had checked his record, they offered him a job mending mattresses. That meant that we had to move to Wilhelmshaven, a town on the North Sea.

27

Tom

1950-1954

Budapest

Challenge

WITH A high honors certificate in my hands, I hoped my dream of becoming an engineer would soon come true. I filled out application forms and mailed them to the only institute I was interested in attending: the Technical University of Budapest, the alma mater of many world class scientists and Nobel laureates.

To my shock and dismay, within a few days, I received a letter from the university informing me of the rejection of my application, without any explanation. I could not believe it and suspected a bureaucratic error. I then spent the entire summer going from one government office to another in an attempt to untangle the situation and locate the source and reason for the rejection. In the process, I often visited the same office and spoke with the same people multiple times. Finally, one official in the Ministry of Education was tired of me and showed me the page in a confidential file where, next to my name, were the following words:

"Capitalist background. Regularly attends mid-week Bible studies. Not to be admitted to any school of higher learning in the country."

"As you can see," the official said, "there is really no sense for you to pursue this matter further. We feel sorry for your pursuit of this hopeless project."

I thanked him for his candor and left, partly crushed, partly relieved. At least I knew where I stood, and the man had saved me from countless additional futile trips. I went home to digest and deal with the situation.

As I closed the door behind me, I suddenly sensed the significance of this revelation, and the collapse of my hope of becoming an engineering student. I sat on the sofa with my eyes fixed on the floor for many long minutes, trying to adjust to this turn of events.

Suddenly, I realized that I had gone through all of this on my own without even consulting God. I slipped down on my knees and asked Him to forgive me and to hold my hand and to lead me to the next step. It took me some time to fall asleep that night.

The next morning, I started with prayer. Then, after some time in thought, I came up with a strange idea.

What if I tried to obtain a job in the university lab as a dishwasher or maintenance helper? I could be near my target, possibly sneak into a few lectures, and most importantly, make a few friends among the staff who might help me get accepted through the back door.

I boarded the streetcar and, within an hour, I stood in front of the university lab foreman asking him for a job.

"If you are so eager to work at the university, maybe you should apply to become a student!" he said.

"Oh what wisdom!" I thought sarcastically. I told him that I had tried all summer without success and hoped to at least work at the place of my dreams.

He went to the phone, talked for a few minutes, then came back and put his hand on my shoulder and said, "Young fellow, go up to the Admitting Office, see the assistant professor. He is willing to talk to you."

The professor was a pleasant-looking young man in his thirties. He offered me a seat and asked me to tell my story. The more I spoke, the more encouragingly he smiled. Then he asked me a few engineering test questions, which I answered as best I could.

"Well," he finished the interview, "you surely would fit in this place, but as you know, the process is rather involved, and the semester starts in two weeks. I'll see what we can do to give you a chance to still apply, but keep your hopes low."

I left the university in a bit of a daze. It had been the first time I had entered the 10,000-person campus, the first time I had walked through corridors with displays of items so close to my heart. Oh, how I yearned to be part of it!

Three days later, I received a letter from the Technical University of Budapest. I could not believe my eyes! It was the letter of acceptance. I was admitted without ever having taken the official entrance examinations.

I dropped to my knees and praised God for this miracle. Two weeks later, I was sitting in the classroom as a full-time student of the Department of Mechanical Engineering – fully financed by the Communist government!

The next four years were a fascinating journey through the sciences and various subjects leading to a diploma in mechanical engineering. As much as I thoroughly disliked high school, I cherished every hour at the university. It was refreshing to study things I was interested in and which, by their technical nature, were free of politics and were taught by real masters whose primary commitment was to get us informed and excited about their subjects.

28

Tom

1950-1954

Rural Hungary

Army

EACH YEAR of university for a month of the summer recess, we had to enlist in the army as a part of compulsory training to become tank officers.

The first year was the toughest, a boot camp starting with a twenty-five mile march in sweltering heat carrying full equipment on our backs.

When I looked at the tall, muscular guys at the front of the line, I wondered how I would stand up to them. During the ten-minute recess each hour, the only respite I allowed myself was to unbutton my top shirt collar. The big guys took the opportunity to sprawl on the ground the moment recess was announced, which caused them more difficulty in getting going when it was time to continue the march. They had muscles, but lacked the discipline and stamina I had been taught as a Boy Scout. In the end, it was I who carried an extra bag for someone who was at the end of his rope.

I entertained myself by blowing the drop of sweat which was just about to fall off the end of my nose onto a leather patch at the center of the flap of the backpack carried by the fellow marching in front of me. I enjoyed improving my skill and aim as we proceeded toward the camp. In the meantime, our squadron deteriorated into a disheveled bunch of limping rookies, yearning for rest and some food. I was very tired but in reasonably good spirits.

Once we arrived and got settled in the tent assigned to us, we had a fairly drab supper saying little to each other. Following that, we were told to line up in an open field where the commanding officer welcomed us and gave us a somber orientation including the location of the medical tent where our sore, wounded feet would be treated the next day. He made no attempt to raise our spirits, even though he could see the shape we were in and knew how we dreaded this whole exercise.

The month of training was characterized by poor food and endless lectures on trivial subjects taught by incompetent officers. The lecturers were ordinary soldiers who knew only a small portion about the tanks and equipment. They were there to make us behave like soldiers and, in a sense, simply to be our guards.

Sunglasses

The toughest challenge was to stay awake for fifty minutes at a time. I thought sunglasses would be a good way to hide my closed eyes but was informed that to wear them during class required medical permission. It took little effort to rub my eyes in the shower prior to a medical visit. The medics fell for the trick.

From then on, I "listened" to the lectures with my eyes closed, my head resting on my wrists. Whenever I could no longer keep my eyes open, I asked my desk mate to nudge me with his elbow when I was asked a question and also to quickly whisper the answer. Most of the time it worked quite well.

Border Patrol

There was a nightly patrol near the Yugoslav border during a period when Stalin had turned against the Yugoslav president Josip Tito. Stalin had called him the "chained dog of the imperialists." Since Hungary was solidly controlled by Russia, a confrontation could have broken out any day.

As I walked the quarter-mile path in the dark with my loaded automatic rifle, every squirrel sounded like an attacking Yugoslav creeping a step closer. It was dark, and it would have been easy to get off the track, wander into enemy territory, and get shot. I figured out a solution. I grabbed a large piece of rotting wood which glowed in the dark with a natural phosphorescence and dropped small pieces of it along the path. For the next two weeks, they served us as path markers.

Driving the Tanks

Learning to drive the T-34 Russian tanks was our only pleasant escape from boredom. We had great fun racing the tanks across fields where we could do no harm. Later on, we sneaked across roads and maneuvered the tanks through forests at times barely missing the trees.

The final test included the thrill of purposefully crashing head-on into a sizeable tree. It was a test of faith in the tank as well as our nerves as we charged ahead, hoping to survive the impending crash. Some of the trainees hit the brakes before crushing the tree, which was cause for failing the qualifications to be a tank driver.

In spite of the numerous aggravations of a few weeks of military life, it did have some redeeming factors. I learned to persevere even when I thought I could not do it anymore, to swallow dumb orders, and to not lose my temper. The strenuous hikes were a good exercise in willpower, tenacity, and camaraderie. And for these few months of our lives, we had no other concern than that of the particular hour, few choices, and no long-range thoughts, although it was for a questionable purpose.

Graduation from Military Training

The day before graduation from military training, we were asked to fill out a four-page questionnaire which included such important questions as, "What was the occupation of your grandfather?" My downfall was a question asking about contacts with the West. I admitted that I was in correspondence with a few people for the purpose of exercising my English.

This was too much for the brass. Within two hours, I was informed of my dishonorable discharge. Not only did I show no regret, but I appeared to be quite happy about this early release. They were visibly upset by my lack of remorse at having lost the opportunity to become an officer. Due to my university education, had I completed the training in good standing, I would have graduated as a lieutenant. I was transported to the train station, my brief career in the People's Army having been terminated.

Military service was the last phase of the engineering education. Despite being discharged, I received my university diploma and was ready and excited to find the career track which would utilize my degree.

29
Jutta
1950-1956
Wilhelmshaven, Germany

Higher Grades

MY FATHER'S job in Wilhelmshaven meant a house of our own but also the challenges of going to new schools and finding new friends.

The city was beautiful with its views of the sea. The land was flat and well-suited to walking and riding bikes. The roads were even designed with bike lanes. There was plenty of activity in the port with large ships delivering their cargo and being loaded with the return shipments.

As with most cities, Wilhelmshaven had been leveled by the carpet bombing of the war. We were given an apartment in a brick house that had been rebuilt. The sea was only a few blocks away from our neighborhood of Altengroden. Our area felt like a village within the greater city. Our house was divided into two apartments. The family that lived in one part was the first in the neighborhood to have a television.

Vati was brilliant at making things from remnants of materials both cloth and metal. He created armchairs for our living room from chairs that had been in an American submarine. We were also given seats from an American Jeep which he turned into dining chairs. He acquired army blankets and turned them into a carpet runner for our hallway. He embroidered the different colors of the blankets together in a pleasing geometric design. The carpet he made for our living room was a rose color with maroon and beige framed with a dark gray. A clock from a U-boat became a table lamp. He built a table as well.

We each had duties around the house. Mine was to beat the dust out of the carpets. First, I would put a kerchief on my head to protect my hair. Then I would take the carpets outside and hang them on a line. I would beat them with the straw beater until there was no longer a cloud of dust with every hit. We girls also had to clean the floors. We were given a gooey liquid soap that we used to scrub the raw wood.

The head of the British command put on a Christmas party. We sang British songs and some German ones. They served a Christmas bread. It was brown and had lots of candied fruit in it. I didn't like it, but I forced myself to eat it. We each received an orange, some nuts, an apple, and cookies as gifts. They were very nice to us.

I entered high school in Wilhelmshaven. There were various options for schools – a Gymnasium, a Mittleschule where the subjects were not as difficult as at the Gymnasium, and a Hauptschule for the lower high school grades. Walter attended the Gymnasium, which was a few miles away. Mutti didn't want me to go that far and enrolled me in the Hauptschule. We rode our bicycles to school. Walter was very protective of us girls. He would come to our school and ride home with us.

Egon was a boy who went to a technical school to become an engineer. He was older than I, but he wanted to spend as much time with me as he could. He would wait so that we could ride home together. There were many times when my bike chain popped. He offered to help and would fix the chain. He would invite me to a café by the ocean. I loved the hot chocolate, but I was not interested in anything romantic.

We had the opportunity to learn a number of languages in school. If you wanted to study history, medicine, or other hard subjects, you needed to study French and Italian. For business, you needed French or Spanish. We all had to take English – we already knew that it would be the world language. I took French and English. We had to read "The Little Prince" in both French and English and write an opinion paper on it. It was my favorite book.

I had a hard time in school. The principal called my parents and said that I needed to go to a school that was not as difficult. I wanted to be a pediatric nurse, but I was too young to start those courses. They put me in the Frauenfachschule, a women's technical college. It combined the basic subjects with practical vocations.

I studied to become a dietitian and a food service manager. I learned how to prepare food for a large number of people. Our studies included planning meals, purchasing food, and managing the staff in the kitchen. For one of the classes, we had to prove what we had learned by producing a meal for forty people.

I got a 1, which was the highest grade, for planning and making a nourishing meal. I had to count what is best for the body, how much you should eat, and how many grams of protein are in it. One of the teachers said, "Jutta, this is brilliant. You did it all right."

I also learned crafts that could be useful in making a home a beautiful place to live. My favorite was painting wooden trays and furniture. Figuring out the designs, preparing the wood, and doing the painting was very satisfying.

I loved the Frauenfachschule. I was so glad my parents took me out of the Hauptschule.

No one would talk to us about the war. We had no idea why we had been fighting, why we had enemies, why we lost, or what the war was about. There was no more talk about us Germans being the "Master Race."

I decided that our history teacher would know. He had served under the Nazis. "I'm very sorry, Miss Merkel," the professor replied, "I am not permitted to talk about this." Another teacher responded with his fingers pretending to zip his lips shut. I asked Mutti, but she also would not say anything.

She would occasionally mention the Jews, always negatively, but she also would not say who they were and why she said these things. She would tell me not to ask so many questions. I began to be suspicious, but realized that no one was going to tell me anything and eventually gave up asking.

I had friends from school. Renate, Kristel, and I were inseparable. We had a wonderful time riding our bikes along the shore, swimming, and giggling over all sorts of conversations.

Another friend was Kristrun. She was a Christian like I had never met before. I noticed that she was different from other friends. Walter became friends with her brother, and he also noticed that there was something special about them.

After I got to know Kristrun, I had two dreams. In one, I was swimming in a lake with many other people. I started to sink. Then I saw Kristrun on an island. She called me, "Jutta, come over here. On this island you will be safe." I swam over the deep, deep water, and when I reached her, I felt safe. I cried and wept after that dream. It was so real.

In another dream, I became a Christian. Many people were laughing as they were swimming in the lake. A soft, nice voice told me that I needed to tell them something important, but I didn't know what the message was. Then I woke up.

When I was fourteen and Walter was fifteen, Mutti decided that she didn't want us to be considered heathen. She signed us up for the confirmation class at the Lutheran church.

The guest at one of the classes was a former POW under the Americans. He spoke of his relationship with God with a deep sense of serenity and assurance. I heard from him that God is alive and that this man had found a lasting means of reaching him. I could see that his joy and peace didn't wear off when church was over. He also talked about the Word as "daily bread" and "living water." I wondered what he was talking about. I thought he must have lost his mind as a prisoner of war.

They gave each of us a special Bible verse. Walter's was that if you are faithful, you will have eternal life.

My course at the Frauenfachschule was four years, but the last year was to be a practicum. There were various jobs I could choose from. The one I took was in the town of Lüneburg, east of Wilhelmshaven. Egon, who had continued to think of himself as my boyfriend, now had a car, and he took us all, Mutti, Vati, and me, to my new work. Mutti and Vati said goodbye as I started my life outside their home.

30

Tom

1954-1956

Budapest

Work

On the Tracks

WITH AN honors diploma in mechanical engineering with a focus on railroad equipment, I looked forward to entering the industry. I had chosen to specialize in railroad equipment engineering because it would encompass most of the disciplines and applications of mechanical engineering. Besides, trains held powerful nostalgic qualities for me.

My application was accepted by Ganz Wagon Works, which employed some 20,000 people and was probably the most advanced industrial organization with the most Western atmosphere in the country. It was prominent in the manufacture of diesel-powered passenger trains and electric locomotives as well as ships, huge generators, and steam turbines. I was happy to be in a company with a great past which still had a bearable present compared with most others.

My first job was inspecting new trains to ensure that they were built according to the engineering drawings and to see that the systems functioned well prior to the test runs. I loved working with both the engineers and the hardy crew of assemblers. At times, we worked through the night crawling under the trains to locate an air leak in the braking system or a malfunction in the heating or electrical control systems. I was known as the dirtiest-looking engineer among the new hires, and that was a compliment.

Assemblers were paid for each job they performed. They had a slip indicating the operation and the compensation they would receive upon approval. Some rugged veterans thought they knew the tasks well enough to not have to consult the drawings. They were upset when I pointed out why the job could not be approved. I looked too young to be the authority. The simple remedy was the growing of a moustache. Within thirty days, I looked a few years older, and it pleased me to see the problem go away.

Train Drivers Course

I was offered a major opportunity to assist a senior engineer in the installation and maintenance of ninety, three-car, high speed trains. The company enrolled me in a four-week train drivers course, the fun I had been dreaming about for quite a while.

During the last two weeks of the course, we performed our duty as uniformed railroad engineers running trains on regular schedules, accompanied by an experienced engineer. While the shift was usually eight hours long, I often accompanied the next engineer for another eight hours if he would let me drive the train. I learned much from these men, including how to avoid killing turkeys that were resting on the tracks! My instructor explained to me that the trick was to not honk the horn when you noticed them. The unusual sound would so stun them that they would raise their heads to try to figure out the source and, in the meantime, would get run over. Not honking the horn, they would get increasingly scared of the rumble and leave the tracks slowly but safely.

My stubborn curiosity could not resist testing the validity of this theory. One day, my instructor became confident enough in my driving skill to retire to his cabin for a quick nap. The moment was perfect for doing the turkey test! All I needed was a bunch of turkeys sitting on the track.

As I was speeding through the colorful countryside, after a curve in the tracks, there were about sixteen turkeys peacefully picking kernels from among the rocks under the track. My heart was thumping, my conscience was hurting, but I pressed the horn button hoping that the turkeys would flee in a hurry, thus proving the theory wrong.

I was shocked to watch how these turkeys did exactly what my instructor warned me about: they stared at my train as we bore down on them. Putting on the brakes was not an option – it would have risked injury to the 100 or so passengers I was transporting. I suffered as I caused the unavoidable massacre as we sped by. I learned the lesson, fortunately, without being caught.

We ended the four, fun-filled weeks with a farewell dinner in a fine restaurant in the center of the town in which we were staying. The local folks had taken us in from the start, and we were sad to part with them. We had enjoyed their hospitality two or three times each week as we relaxed after work.

Back in the factory, the work took on new meaning. I conducted experiments which resulted in figuring out why the wheels of high-speed trains had a chronic problem of skidding when the brakes lowered the speed. I found that brake pressure had to be reduced automatically. This resulted in a redesign of the brake system.

I knew I was in the right field of work.

31

Jutta

1956-1957

Lüneburg, Germany

Internship

LÜNEBURG WAS in the farmland south of Hamburg. It had not been bombed during the war, and it still had its old houses and city buildings. This may have been why it was chosen to have a center for people who had been traumatized by the war. It was the Nord-Ostdeutsche Akademie. I became the manager of the kitchen for the Akademie, arranging for three meals every day and overseeing the kitchen helpers. I got paid very little, but I did not need much. I had a three-room suite – a living room, bedroom, and bathroom – in the Akademie building.

I was surprised to find that Tante Luci was a manager at the Akademie. I had not seen her since we escaped from Poland, eleven years before. She knew me only as the niece who had lived in her house.

I remembered that she had hit me for being afraid of a mouse. It had been during an afternoon naptime. A mouse ran across my bed. I screamed and jumped out of the bed, knocking over a beautiful Asian vase that was standing on the floor. It shattered. Tante Luci hit me and ordered me never again to scream when I saw a mouse.

Now we had to work together as adults. Officially, my position as the manager of the kitchen made me her assistant. She was kind to me. We did not talk about Poland. She never told me why Onkel Hans was not there in Lüneburg.

The patients came from everywhere. They came for a few weeks to meet with the doctors and professors to learn how to live again. There were both soldiers and civilians. They poured out their hearts, and some of them cried.

One man talked to me about his experiences. He cried right away and said, "I cannot live anymore like this."

I said, "Bit by bit, day by day, you will feel better. You can talk to me or a professor."

Sometimes I would make them a cup of tea. I just befriended them. In some of the group sessions, we sang German folk songs together.

We took one of the groups on a bus to a border between East and West Germany. The bus driver told us to be careful what we said to the East German guards when we would cross a certain bridge. The Communist soldier on the bridge stood legs apart looking very scary.

We wanted to make a connection with them because they were Germans, too, but on the other side of the border. We started singing "Im Früling" ("In the Spring"). We wanted to make the people on the Com-munist side know that we did not hate them. Singing songs is a wonderful thing. It builds bridges between people.

There were activities and events for different groups who came as patients. Some came from the Baltic states. My mother had grown up in Estonia, of a large, wealthy family with lots of relatives. One event was a beautiful dinner, and there was dancing afterward, a real Baltic ball.

Mutti had loaned me a black silk skirt and a white blouse with a collar. It was beautiful, but she did not tell me that the skirt had a rip in it. I danced a Strauss waltz, and my partner stepped on the skirt, ripping it further. I had safety pins and went to the bathroom to fix it. When I came out, he said it didn't matter since we are all cousins!

The next day, someone wanted to take a picture of all of the people there who were of my family's clan. I wore an outfit that I had made – a blue skirt and vest and a white blouse. It had silver buttons around the top of the skirt that attached to the buttons around the hem of the vest. The buttons together looked like a belt. Everyone asked me where I had bought it. I didn't want to tell them that I had made it because I didn't want to make another for them.

One of my closer cousins was there. She and I got together for bike rides and other fun. Our conversations were natural and funny. We became good friends.

I spent four weeks of that year with severe pneumonia. There was no hospital, no x-rays. A neighbor took me to the doctor. He checked me out and said that there was nothing more he could do for me except for telling me to put hot compresses on my chest. A few days later, the doctor came in with some big tablets and told me to chew one several times a day. I started to get better after that. I was in my room recuperating for a month. When I needed fresh air, they would open my window.

(The tablets were one of the first antibiotics.)

There was a boy whom I had met at one of the activities who knew which was my window. He tied a note to a stone and threw it in. It landed on my bed. The note read, "When can I see you? I miss you so much." I was surprised but not at all interested in anything romantic.

One of my jobs was to seat people as they came into the dining room. One day, I looked down the list of patients coming in. I saw the name of my best friend in Poland. When she came to the front of the line, I asked her if she truly was my friend. I looked at her leg and saw the scar from when our dog Lux had bitten her. She was the one I was playing with when I stepped on the thorn. We hugged and cried. It didn't matter that everyone was watching. That night we stayed in a barn so that we could stay up late and not disturb anyone. We talked for most of the night about what had happened to our families since we had last seen each other.

I had a sweet girlfriend who lived in the town. Babette was the daughter of one of the professors at the Akademie. They had a house to themselves in the town. We went together to Johanneskirche, the medieval cathedral in the center of the city where the organist played concerts. My favorites were when he played Bach. The church had fantastic acoustics.

My year ended with graduation from the Frauenfachschule. My diploma meant I could work as a dietitian and food service manager wherever I could get a job.

32

Jutta

1957-1959

Mülheim, Germany

Work

I READ about a job at a YMCA in the city of Mülheim. This was in the industrial, coal-mining district near the border with The Netherlands. Düsseldorf, Duisburg, Essen, and their universities were also nearby. The YMCA housed 200 workers and students.

I took the train to Mülheim and presented myself to the Lehmanns, the managers of the YMCA. They hired me immediately. I ran the kitchen, planned the menus, ordered the food, and oversaw the preparation.

We had a few problems. I bought big chunks of beef at the butcher, but once when we started to heat it in the pan, maggots crawled out. We had to throw it all away. Another time, the drain in the kitchen sink was clogged. Everyone on the kitchen crew tried to clean it, but with no success. They didn't want me to try since I was the dietitian and shouldn't have to do such work. I did it anyway, and I got it clean. They gave me a certificate for helping. It was a fun time!

I never had a problem with my helpers. No matter how messy the job – cleaning and deboning fish or the cleaning of the kitchen – they always said, "Gerne." ("With pleasure.")

We had students from all over the world. Occasionally, I learned about their food. One morning when I got up at 5:00 a.m. to make the coffee and tea, there was a bowl on the table in the kitchen of what looked like nice plums. I bit into one expecting it to be sweet and juicy. Whatever they were, they caused an awful burning in my throat. Instead of a plum, it was an olive. When the Arab student came in, he said, "Did you eat one? I got them for you."

One of the students was from Indonesia. He took me out on dates. On one of them he ordered soup. He didn't tell me until I had eaten most of it that it was made of shark. I nearly threw up on the table! He gave me a brooch. It was a silver and onyx sword and sheath. They were attached to each other by a chain, and the sword fit perfectly into the sheath. He must have thought we would get married someday because he said, "If you don't marry me, throw it away."

I said to myself, "Don't do that to me. I am not going to marry you."

I asked Mutti, "Why won't the guys leave me alone?"

Mutti said, "Well, Jutta, you are old enough to say something."

The manager of the YMCA was Hartmut Lehmann. He and his wife Elisabet and their five children lived in a small apartment on the floor above mine. They took me in as a family member. When I had the afternoon or evening off, they would invite me to dinner and include me in whatever they were doing. They welcomed me to sit in their living room to write letters and listen to the radio. If Mr. and Mrs. Lehmann needed to go out, I was happy to take care of the children.

They even took me along on their vacations. Somehow, we all would fit into their four-person car. When we went to the mountains, we took a picnic – sandwiches and coffee if it was available. Everything was skimpy, but we had enough.

The children were sweet and kind. Mr. and Mrs. Lehmann never yelled at them, but they obeyed. If one of the children did something bad, they would take that child aside and talk to him.

Mr. Lehmann had lost his legs to Russian grenades during the war. He had wooden legs that he buckled on with leather straps over his shoulders. He loved to swim. He would take off his legs, and Elisabet and I would carry him to the water. He could swim very well with his arms. When he was ready to come out, he would wiggle himself out onto the sand, and we would help him put on his legs. He never complained.

Mrs. Lehmann had an old sewing machine. She sewed all of their clothes and curtains. She knit all of their socks. She was a very busy but very joyful person.

She and Mr. Lehmann would pray before the meals. Once they asked me to pray. I was so nervous I was sweating. I said something like, "Thank you for this food. Amen."

I always prayed by myself at night. "Lieber Gott, mach mich Fromm, das ich zu dir in dem Himmel komm." ("Dear God, make me holy, that I will come to you in heaven.") I don't know where I got this prayer, maybe from my grandmother.

The Lehmanns were different, and I wanted what they had. I couldn't grasp what it was. They never complained about the difficulties in their lives. Instead, I saw only peace and joy. I remembered having the same feeling when I had listened to the man who led my confirmation class many years before.

I finally got up the courage to ask them, "What is it that you have? Where does it come from?" They said it came from Jesus Christ, God's Son. They invited me to come to a Bible study. I said no. I could only think of what I had been taught, that such things are for the lame, the blind, and the weak.

They kept inviting me, and finally I gave in and agreed to go. I was surprised to find that the evening was really enjoyable. The Lehmanns finally explained their "special ingredient." They said that what I was missing was salvation through Jesus Christ. No one had ever told me that I could have a personal relationship with Jesus. They spent time going through the Bible, teaching me about the Son of God who had come to earth to save mankind from their sin.

I also heard this message at a rally in Essen. A friend invited me to come with her and her husband to a meeting led by Wilhelm Busch, a German pastor. I was impressed with his life story, his preaching, and all he said about Jesus Christ. My friend also took me to a gathering led by an American, Norvel Young. One of the songs they sang was "Just as I Am." It said that Jesus accepts us just as we are. I knew that that could not be true for me, but it was starting to sink in that there was a different life available through Jesus Christ.

When the movie "The Ten Commandments" was showing in the city, the Lehmanns took me along to see it. I had heard very little about the Old Testament, and I was fascinated. I bought myself a Bible to read these stories for myself. All that I was learning was adding to my understanding of the Bible and its message.

During the two years with the Lehmanns at the YMCA in Mülheim, I was considering moving away from Germany. Vati had always encouraged us to see the world to get a new view of life. I did not want to move back with my parents and could not see myself staying on in

Mülheim. I started to look for opportunities in other countries.

A job offer came from the ambassador of Germany to Australia. Australia sounded like a wonderful place. The ambassador's wife was blind. The job was to be their nanny and also be her driver. I did not drive and was too scared to take the job. It also was too far away.

Instead, I started to look toward America. One of the requirements in the application for a visa for the United States was to have a medical examination. The doctors found a spot on my lungs, which they interpreted as exposure to tuberculosis. I was refused a visa. Canada was advertising a need for nannies, and immigrants from Germany were welcome. Their medical examination was not as strict, and I received the immigration papers.

Before I left the Lehmanns, they told me that Canada had many churches of many denominations. Before that, I only knew that there were Roman Catholics and Lutherans. They told me to look for a church that had Jesus at its center. That would be more important than its name.

33

Tom

October 1956

Budapest

Revolution

ON OCTOBER 23, 1956, word spread in Budapest that the Hungarian Writers Association was planning a major gathering downtown in Heroes' Square. The purpose would be to discuss solidarity with writers who sought less censorship and an atmosphere of free expression.

That morning, as my friends and I were taking the streetcar to the train drivers course, we overheard other riders telling each other the news of the gathering. We agreed that instead of going home, we should go to see what it was all about.

My two colleagues and I found it unusually hard to concentrate that day. Even the instructor appeared to be distracted. Our minds were on Heroes' Square where, for the first time in ten years, a non-Communist-organized public gathering was to take place.

After work, we bought sandwiches and beers and headed to the giant square. About 5,000 people had already gathered.

"Russians go home!"

"Down with Communism!"

"We want freedom!"

We stood about 150 feet from the forty-foot-tall bronze statue of Stalin.

Someone yelled, "Let's pull him down!"

A roar of approval followed. A roll of steel cable was tossed to the ground. About twenty of us grabbed the cable, and a few athletic types lifted it and tied it around the dictator's neck.

We pulled the ropes tight, but the statue did not budge. We noticed that a truck had pulled up close to us. We asked the driver to let us tie the cable to the truck's towing hitch. He jumped out to help. Once the cable was in place, we pushed the truck to help it pull the cable. Stalin stood firm.

Someone shouted, "Get a welder!"

Within minutes, a welder climbed up to the statue, lit his torch, and made a big incision on Stalin's legs behind the knees. The driver put the truck in low gear and slowly released the clutch. The cable lifted from the ground and tightened. We watched breathlessly as the giant bronze image of Stalin slowly started to bend forward. At first, it appeared to be making a polite bow, but as it progressed, the big dictator just about jumped off his pedestal leaving behind only his two feet cut off below the knees.

We broke out in applause.

Someone inserted Hungarian flags into the hollow legs. The flags had holes in the middle where the Communist emblem had been cut out.

I said goodbye to my two buddies and took the streetcar home. Everybody was discussing the recent events with shining eyes. Some suggested openly that the next step should be to get rid of the Communists altogether.

I turned on the radio when I got home. People had started to converge on the Radio Budapest building in spite of threats by the secret police. I could hardly wait to leave and get there, but Mother fell ill from her fears of the uprising. I stayed with her and followed the events over the radio.

I heard that the crowd swelled to tens of thousands and that people sang banned patriotic songs. I learned that after listening to the fiery speeches of popular writers, the demonstrators demanded that the whole gathering be put on the radio – live. The guards at the radio station surrendered, and then I heard the news as it was aired to the rest of the country.

A beautiful spirit greeted us the next day. Everywhere we could see the Hungarian flag with the hole in the middle. Most of the illuminated red stars on buildings were gone. It was if a decade-long winter had given way to the sights, sounds, and smell of spring! There were happy faces everywhere.

We went to work hoping to find out what would be the next step. I knew life would not be normal, but I wanted to make sure that I would get the week's salary.

Russian Crackdown

At daybreak on the morning of November 3, we awoke to a sound we had last heard in 1945 – the sound of artillery in action. I jumped out of bed and looked out at the deserted streets of the sleeping city. Occasionally, a Hungarian military truck, followed later by tanks, sped by. They were loaded with youths holding guns. I learned that mobilized and formidable Soviet divisions were approaching the city, and these youths were ready to face them.

I simply could not believe this! It could not be possible that our dream would be crushed so cruelly and so soon.

Premier Nagy's last words on the radio still ring in my ears, "I must inform you, the Soviet forces were instructed to crush our new system. I and my government have sounded all the rescue signals we could to the world, but we have to realize there is little hope that the West will risk getting into a war for the freedom of one small nation. I sign off with the hope that one day freedom will return to this land." These last words came from a man choked with emotion. He knew he himself would be the first target of the brutal hands of the returning Communist regime.

With great sadness, life started again.

Public transportation became nonexistent. The only way to cover any significant distance was to hitchhike. When that failed, I waited at busy street corners for open trucks that had stopped at the traffic policeman's signal. I jumped on and rode as long as the truck was going in the direction of my destination. If it turned off, I hoped that the next traffic policeman would not be too far off. Often, I would end up farther from the plant than when I started out, but eventually, even if it took four or five "transfers," I managed to get to work in the morning and then back home at the end of the day.

We were all so disillusioned that work appeared as a futile, insignificant activity serving only one purpose – a paycheck at the end of the week. Life seemed hopeless, and the future seemed to be dull, if not outright dark as the days were swallowed by cold November nights.

After the Russians crushed the Nagy regime, 150,000 people took a bagful of their essential belongings and fled the country. I had no desire to stay, but I could not help wondering whether God wanted me to serve Him there, behind the Iron Curtain, or if He had plans for me in the free world.

Influence of Others

Every day when I arrived at work, I heard of another colleague who had left the country. I looked at my co-workers and wondered if they would show up the next day.

A few days after the Communists had reasserted their power, an experienced, good-humored co-worker put his hands on my shoulders, looked squarely into my eyes, and told me that he would be very disappointed if I missed this opportunity to leave the country.

"Why are you still here? You are smart. I will be disappointed if you show up any more."

Another day he asked, "Are you still here? What's wrong with you?"

Those few words pushed me into giving the idea of escaping serious thought. That night, I tried to sleep, but I could not turn my mind off. At times, I felt it would be a cop-out, fleeing from difficulty and deserting my fellow Christians who were living under persecution for their faith. On the other hand, I wondered if I would be recognized in photos or films taken at the site of Stalin's statue. At other times, I could not help believing that God could use my talents better in a free world.

I had a good diploma from a world-renowned university, spoke fluent English, German, and French, and was a tourist at heart. However, a clear thought came to me. If I managed to escape to the West and then simply lived a self-serving life, I would not have fulfilled God's will.

Would I see Mother again? Would I see the city of Budapest and my favorite spots in the country again? Would I ever again see my friends and my cousins? All the memories swelled up and swept over me in waves.

Just when I thought that the decision was clear, the doubts came charging at me. I prayed for guidance, but I could not see the answer. After several hours, the first glimmer of dawn appeared. I had to come to a decision. I felt that if I tried to follow God, I could not end up in defeat.

Counsel of Emil Hajós

I decided to seek the counsel of Emil Hajós. After a time of intense prayer together, I realized that escaping with Mother was beyond her physical ability. She was comfortable in her job and in her apartment. It appeared that the right thing for me was to leave the country. Emil listened to my plan and nodded approvingly. We hugged each other for the last time.

Mother took the decision gracefully, and while she had tears in her eyes, she did not hold me back. She knew that we might never see one another again, either because I would not make it safely to Austria or because she would not be allowed to follow me. I packed a few essentials in my briefcase: my engineering diploma, a compass, my

Bible, a hunter's knife, my hygiene set, and one change of clothes. After a last hug and prayer, I left with a lump in my throat.

I bought a pint of rum in a flat bottle in order to have a supply of sufficient warmth and calories in case I would have to hide lying in snow for an extended period. I headed to the circular artery of the city and jumped onto the back of the first truck that stopped at the intersection. Fortunately, it carried me just a bit past the South Railway Station, the terminal for trains heading south and west. After a few minutes' walk, I stood at the ticket counter and opened the small linen bag that was tucked inside my shirt. The bag hung on a short string around my neck, a safe way to keep it hidden and avoid losing it as I jumped on and off the trucks. It contained the equivalent of thirty-four dollars.

With ticket in hand, I walked to the designated track where the conductor answered my question before I asked it, "Yes, my friend, this is the train to Vienna."

The humor of his answer was that the train service from Budapest to Vienna had not existed for decades. Hungarian trains stopped at the border. The few passengers who had permission to travel to the West went through a thorough screening before they were allowed to board the Austrian train waiting on the other side of the border.

Soon he blew his whistle, smiled, and announced, "Budapest to Vienna. Please close the car doors." He lifted his signal, and the train started rolling.

I had a last look at Budapest from the open platform. It was my hometown and a beautiful city, yet I didn't have any tears in my eyes. I was leaving behind too many bad experiences.

34

Tom

November 1956

Budapest to the Austrian Border

Escape

I ENTERED a passenger compartment and found all of the seats occupied. I had to go through several cars before I found a place. People discussed border-crossing plans openly, maps spread before them. The secret police appeared to be tucked away for this period. No one would have thought of attempting escape in such an obvious way if the police were active. My alibi, just in case, was an address near the border of a former classmate whom I would say that I planned to visit.

The idea was to get close enough to the border by train so that it would be a manageable walk of the last ten to twelve miles. Most people had an appointment with a farmer near the border or planned to join other people who knew one. These men and women were making a terrific business guiding dissidents across the border. Most of them did an honest job at high risk to themselves. Others, a very few, took the money and disappeared in the darkness, leaving their compatriots wondering where to go, often into the arms of the Russian border patrol.

It was a two-hour train ride.

At the border town, I joined a group of about forty led by a farmer's wife. We started around 7:00 p.m.

We must have walked an hour when I passed a fifty-year-old lady sitting on one of her two large suitcases. There was a frightened, desperate look in her eyes. I let my group walk ahead and stopped for a few minutes to see if there was a chance I could help her.

She said, "Nobody can help me." She was totally exhausted and had decided to sit there until the border patrol would find her and ship her back to a jail or shoot her on the spot. She had a successful son in New York who had arranged for relatives in Vienna to pick her up once she crossed the border.

Lifting her suitcases one by one, I realized why she was so exhausted. I asked her to open them. She was not only carrying her best clothing, but framed pictures, souvenirs, and a variety of "precious possessions." I told her she had to choose between getting rid of half of her luggage or losing her chance to see her son again. Her tears rolled down as she watched me scatter her precious possessions on the wet grass in the middle of the forest. Soon, instead of two heavy suitcases, we had one which was of reasonable weight. To my surprise, she showed little resistance. She had just needed someone to separate her from some of her treasured load. A few minutes later, we were walking together, she carrying her purse and I carrying my briefcase and the remains of her wealth. I dictated a slow pace at first but changed to a stronger one once I noticed that the lady had come back to herself mentally and physically.

Despite being separated from my group and guided only by my compass, I was amazed by the peace I had. I felt the presence of God in that quiet forest on that dark December night not knowing how close we might be to a Russian border patrol hiding behind the bushes.

Since we were walking in a dense forest and I was not eager to walk with only my new-found companion, we did not stop until we caught up with my group. We continued together and without noticing it, I began humming the tunes of my favorite hymns. One of them was "Onward Christian Soldiers." My new friends thought that maybe I had lost my senses. I shared with them that I walked with Someone who was very present in all situations and was able to fill one's heart with joy and peace even in tricky circumstances.

Russian Border Patrol

We were getting very close to the border. The terrain grew less dense, and blinding flares exposed us enough that we hugged the ground every time one appeared, sometimes as often as one every two minutes.

Soon after one of the flares went up, we found ourselves surrounded by a group of grim-looking Russian border policemen. We thought that this was the end of our hopes of crossing the border. We decided to attempt to bribe them. The ladies removed their necklaces, bracelets, some even their wedding rings. Men handed over their watches, silver pencils, cameras and, of course, cigarettes. I was not prepared to part with my watch, but I presented one of them with my half-pint bottle of rum. It brought a sparkle to the soldier's eyes and a bright smile to his face as he took a gulp before he passed it on to his buddies. They were distracted from collecting their loot as they anticipated how much may be left in the bottle when it would be their turn.

Once the transaction was over, they not only allowed us to continue but also pointed out the direction where we would have the least chance of meeting another Russian patrol. This was not just charity. If we were to meet another patrol, they would conclude that the first patrol had relieved us of our valuables which, at least on paper, was a punishable offense. If one considers that approximately 150,000 Hungarians escaped within a four-week period, those Russian soldiers must have had a pretty good harvest. They wished us a safe journey, and we continued toward our goal, hoping to not have another surprise before reaching the border.

No Man's Land

After spotting a few more flares, we noticed a watch-tower in the distance. It was still dark enough that the comrades were using the flares to keep an eye on the roughly 150-foot-wide bare stretch, a "no man's land" between Austria and Hungary. Instead of risking potentially violent encounters in the dense forests, they figured it was simpler to gun down the escapees while they crossed this open area.

It must have been about 4:00 a.m. when we arrived at this strip of land. We stopped for a while, partly because we could not believe that we had actually made it to a point where we could see trees rooted in the soil of the free world. We just stared at the trees and at each other. Our faces reflected excitement, anticipation, and that strange feeling which precedes an action in which you will either make it or lose everything that links you to this world. I was really not afraid of a bullet in my head, but I dreaded the thought of being wounded badly enough to be dragged away and beaten up before being transferred to a jail – or into eternity.

We discussed the strategy of crossing the no-man's-land. Considering the limited reach of the searchlights, we figured that it was unlikely the tower patrol would be able to survey continuously the entire mile or two assigned to them.

We thought we would have the best chance if we sprinted across in four quick bursts. We decided to spread out, lining up along a sixty-foot line four rows deep. Those who had little children put them closest to men who had a free hand or into knapsacks with room for a little one.

When we were ready and we were surrounded by silence, we could sense our heartbeats. One of us yelled with a muffled voice, "Run!" The race was on to freedom or death.

It was amazing to see how fast a middle-aged lady could run if her life depended on it! And it was the same with old men, women, and small children. It appeared that all physical handicaps, if there were any, were temporarily lifted as we passed from the territory of oppression to freedom.

To our joy, we were on the other side without a single flare or bullet disturbing our escape. Knowing the Russians, we did not feel safe even on Austrian soil, so we kept running as fast and as far as we could without looking back. I stayed with the last of the four groups, so I could be sure that the lady traveling with me would make it over before me.

As we emerged from the Austrian border-forest area, I spotted a building in the misty distance. As we got closer, I started to decipher the message on a sign above the door: "Lebensmittel." Food store! The sign was in German. The escape had seemed so peaceful that some of us had wondered if the "no-man's-land" was possibly only one of several to be crossed. Now we knew we were truly in Austria!

Austria

We walked toward the building and met the first Austrian border patrol. They greeted us with a cheerful "Guten Morgen" ("good morning") and directed us to the refugee camp in the border town of Lutzmannsburg.

When we got there, we stood in long lines before the desks of immigration officials who recorded our names and issued us temporary Austrian refugee-resident permits. Good hot soup was waiting for us in the next room, and along with the food, smiling volunteers gave each of us a navy-blue plastic bag with UNITED STATES ESCAPEE PROGRAM printed on the side. In it were essential items for hygiene: toothbrush, toothpaste, shaving cream, a brass Gillette razor, towel, soap, sewing kit, comb – the result of donations of many Americans. This kit was most helpful because those of us equipped for hiking and camping had not necessarily brought along supplies sufficient for living in barracks for an extended period of time.

We were told we could expect to stay in the barracks for four to six weeks before our applications to the country of our final destination would be processed. It sounded like a long time, but we had a truly open schedule. I hoped to get outside the camp gates and experience a bit of Vienna as a tourist.

I took an available bed in one of the barracks and lay down on top of the blanket. Taking off my boots, I tied the laces to my wrists to ensure they wouldn't walk away while I rested. I closed my eyes without trying to figure out what would be next and dozed off into a deep sleep.

A few minutes into my nap, I was awakened by a tap on my shoulder and a timid voice.

"Tom, would you do one more favor for me?" It was the lady I had helped cross the border. "Would you call this number? They are my relatives, waiting for my call so they can pick me up and take me to Vienna. They speak only German, which I don't."

I rubbed my eyes, put on my boots, got up, and looked for an official who would let us know if this was possible. He said it was no problem as long as she was willing to take care of herself and arrange her own journey to her destination. The lady had no concerns, so I phoned her relatives and informed them of her arrival. They were delighted to hear the news and said that they would be in Lutzmannsburg within two hours in their car.

Two hours later, well-dressed Dr. Mayer accompanied by his wife arrived and found the lady. They embraced each other and after a few words of discussion, Dr. Mayer asked me if I would be interested in coming along for the ride to Vienna as their way of appreciation for helping the lady cross the border.

We were released in a few minutes.

Tom – November 1956

Just a few hours after running across no-man's-land, I was sitting in the front seat of a posh Mercedes speeding toward Vienna!

We stopped for supper in a roadside restaurant for what seemed like a royal meal. Arriving in Vienna in early evening, Dr. Mayer put me up in a simple but nice hotel, paid for the room for two days and gave me 200 schillings for necessities – a little fortune for a single refugee. He thanked me one more time for helping the lady cross the border, and I in turn thanked him for his generosity.

35

Tom

November 1956 - January 1957

Vienna, Austria

Freedom

God works in wonderful ways. How could I have planned this chain of events?

LESS THAN a day after crossing the border, I spread out my belongings in a clean hotel room, washed my only change of clothes in the bathtub, and crawled into bed, praising God. I did not give a single thought to tomorrow. I hit the bed and let the world run its affairs without me for a full fourteen hours.

I woke up in broad daylight having missed the complimentary continental breakfast. I got dressed and went out to find my own breakfast. I bought a few rolls, butter, good Austrian sausages, and a bunch of bananas at a grocery store nearby. I felt rich and free as I walked back to the hotel.

Only then did it occur to me that all this time my mother must have been ceaselessly praying for my safety. I had a look at the food in my bag but resisted the temptation and went instead to the receptionist to see if I could call Mother. Within minutes, she was on the phone and was delighted to learn that all had gone well. Both of us were careful about the content of the conversation, not knowing who might be secretly listening. The last thing I wanted was to get her into trouble in case some agency planned to exert pressure on relatives of recent dissidents. She appeared to overcome her loneliness with the knowledge that I was looking forward to a brighter and safer future than if I had stayed at home. I promised to keep her posted at least once a week unless I managed to get on a boat to cross the Atlantic sooner than expected. We had a brief word of prayer and said goodbye to each other. It was a great feeling to have assured her of my safety and my concern for her.

Following a most enjoyable brunch in my hotel room, I asked myself the obvious question: What is the next step? After a relaxed time of reading the Bible and prayer with God, I put my mind into second gear: Where am I? Where should I go?

I first had to be sure that I had a place to stay after my prepaid hotel bill ran out. The hotel operator helped me locate the refugee center in the city. A few minutes later, I was on my way. I decided to take advantage of the situation and promoted myself from the lowly status of refugee to the adventurous position of a tourist.

It was exciting to see well-dressed people walking around with rosy cheeks and shining eyes – free, not dominated by authorities, masters of their own destinies. I had lived under oppression for so long that this caught my attention immediately. The entire city radiated freedom, purpose and vibrant life, a new world for me after the drab decade following the war. I could not help noticing the cleanliness of streetcars and buses, the neat markings and signs on the streets, the shop windows displaying quality merchandise. It reminded me of the time when Budapest was called the Paris of Central Europe.

We cannot fully realize darkness until we are exposed to light or fully realize oppression until exposed to freedom. Likewise, we cannot appreciate fully the beauty and value of light or freedom unless we experience a period of darkness or oppression.

The tragedy of Communism was that people eventually got used to drabness, neglect, dysfunction, and to the authority of others interfering in one's life without legal justification. Once people get used to this, their children, never having seen a different lifestyle, assume that this is the normal way of life. Soon most people become slaves to the government and no longer resist the system to which they are subjected.

Refugee Center

After a good half hour walk, I arrived at the refugee center staffed by Austrians, Hungarian refugees, and volunteers from all over the globe. I received an ID card, which would provide me with free or heavily discounted necessities, including transportation, meal coupons, and a modest but sufficient weekly allowance.

Taking a good look at the list of refugees, I located the address and phone number of my friend John, the electrical engineer who had been one of the persuasive forces in my leaving Hungary. Within minutes, John's familiar voice was on the phone. He already had accommodations provided by one of the refugee aid groups and suggested that we get together and settle my future as quickly as possible.

He was an old hand in this situation, having escaped two weeks before I did. We arranged that I would share his room in a modest guesthouse.

I checked out of the hotel Dr. Mayer had provided for me and moved in with John. To make things simple, we agreed that every space on the left and on the bottom would be mine, and everything on the right and on the top would be John's.

Now we had to settle where we should establish our future. While we had the choice of staying there, the number of new settlers had to be limited in this small country. I also reasoned that staying so close to the Red Army made little sense after all the years I spent under their control.

I wanted to go to an English-speaking country since I spoke fluent English. Also, from what I had read or had seen in the movies during the forties, I generally liked the Anglo-Saxon style and character.

John had signed up to go to Australia and had filled out an advance form for me also even before I left Hungary. I had two problems with his choice: among all the nations which had offered homes to Hungarians, Australia had one of the least advantageous ratios between males and females. While getting married soon was not on my agenda, I was hoping I would have a choice without unreasonably fierce competition once I got tired of being a bachelor.

The second problem was the distance. I wanted to be close to American advanced technology and not too far from Europe, but I was afraid of the immenseness, the fast pace, and clamor I perceived in the United States. I did not like posters and movies from Hollywood that projected crime, loud music, conflicts between blacks and whites, and the excessive rush after money and status.

Unfortunately, this was the image that many, if not most, people who had never visited the United States carried in their minds. I suggested to John that we go to Canada. It had plenty of space, a need for immigrants, beautiful scenery, a slower pace, yet was close to America. John concurred.

We were received warmly at the Canadian embassy, and after a brief check of our backgrounds and education, we were told that the door was open for us. It was good news, and after having canceled the Australia applications, we were looking forward to a future in Canada. We had great peace about this choice and decided to enjoy our few remaining days in Vienna with a very limited budget but with a fair amount of imagination.

Tourists

John and I were like the "odd couple" of the film I watched years later. We could not have been more different. What bound us together was the years we spent together as Boy Scouts in the same patrol and our common situation in Austria. We also enjoyed seeing new things, good music, sports, and had great fun teasing each other. That is, I had great fun teasing him!

John was very skillful at finding out where we could get extra supplies, where they were issuing used clothing, or where we could attend a free concert. Usually, he made these arrangements when it was the time to prepare a meal, do the dishes, or clean the room. Consequently, I became quite skilled in the manual aspects of our existence, which John thoroughly appreciated.

Briefcase

We carried our bag lunch, a camera, and other essentials in a briefcase. Initially, I carried the briefcase, and John carried the map and the sightseeing instructions. He was the pilot, and I was the mobile depot. As the days went on, John inserted more and more "essentials" into the briefcase, which, of course, I carried. Being grateful for his assistance in getting established in Vienna, I did not object to being the laborer as long as it was reasonable. However, the briefcase got heavier every day, and my arms were getting increasingly sore by the time we got home in the evenings.

One night, I suggested that the next day we take turns carrying the briefcase. To make things simple, I suggested he carry the briefcase during the even hours while I would do the lugging during the odd hours. John accepted the proposal but without any visible sign of enthusiasm.

He was still the expert on sightseeing, and planned our trips meticulously. I noticed with interest that our trips on the following days started and ended on odd hours. It appeared a strange coincidence that whenever we traveled by streetcar or had a meal or sat down on a bench in a park, it usually occurred during the hours when John was supposed to carry the bag. The rascal got away with half the strain no matter how good the system I suggested seemed to be. It took me about a week to realize this was a partnership of equal rights but unequal load, and it was time to steer our coexistence to a more balanced format.

I assisted John with reporting the streets and squares we crossed. He then checked the map, got the coordinates, and located our position. I think I was quite a help to him, having good eyes and a good sense for where street signs may be found. In one case, however, I was unable to resist the temptation to give John a little challenge. I told him we are at the corner of Maria-Hilferstrasse and Einbahn-strasse. John had no problem finding Maria-Hilferstrasse, but even after several scans of the list under "E," he could not find Einbahnstrasse.

"Look again, John," I encouraged him, "You are an ace. I have confidence in you. You will find it in a minute."

At this point, my conscience, which often failed me when I did pranks, kicked in.

"Oh my goodness, John," I pretended to apologize. "I just realized Einbahnstrasse means 'one way.' No wonder you could not find it under "E." *(It is just as it would be futile to find "one way" under "O" on an English map.)* "Look up 'Bundgasse' instead!"

Quoting his response would be out of place in this gentle-mannered story and would embarrass him if he reads it.

New Year's Eve

It was New Year's Eve. We met two girls at the refugee center and asked them to accompany us for the evening. What do two young fellows and two girls do with a budget that would finance a big night at McDonald's as long as the meal plan did not exceed a hamburger, French fries, and a Coke?

By now, I felt very much at home in Vienna. As we walked toward the center of the city, I asked the porter of a hotel what he would do if he had our budget. He suggested we go the Augustiner Keller and sit down at a table where there is room, hopefully next to some friendly people.

"Order a pair of Vienna sausages, and see what happens. People love to make friends on New Years' Eve, particularly if they are just a couple or two hoping for additions to their party."

This sounded good to me. We entered the hall. Not a single space anywhere! Suddenly, a large group stood up and prepared to leave. There were at least twelve chairs around the table. We darted to it and ordered our meal for the night, hoping for the best.

Soon another couple arrived and asked us if we minded if they sat with us. We gladly obliged. They turned out to be a lot of fun, and soon there was good laughter at the table. The only concern was how rapidly our sausages seemed to get shorter, the buns smaller, and the single bottle of beer emptier. We did not lose hope, but just kept eating smaller bites to make them last longer.

Within an hour, our table was full, and we had to add another small table to accommodate more people. It was a common gesture on this occasion for couples to take turns ordering for the group both food and drinks. We had told them about our lack of wealth early enough so that they skipped us each time. They designated the night as a New Year's Eve celebration of the Hungarian cause of freedom.

We appreciated the solidarity, taught them a few cheerful Hungarian songs, joined them in singing Austrian favorites while swinging arm in arm, toasted everybody and every cause we could think of, and enjoyed the food and drinks without ever having to open our flat wallets.

Before we knew it, it was 4 a.m. and time to go home. We hugged, kissed, and cheered as we said goodbye and wished one another a Happy New Year. Everyone was in high spirits, especially John. He had had a bit too much of the good Bavarian beer and suggested that we march home like soldiers. The rest of us preferred to walk normally on the abandoned streets covered with fresh snow, and savored the fresh morning air after the best New Year's Eve celebration we had ever had.

We dropped the girls off and headed home. Once we slipped into our hotel room, John spent quite a bit of time in the bathroom and most of the rest of the day in bed.

Mount Semmering

A couple of hours later, I took a shower and left for the bus, which took me to the beautiful Mount Semmering, the site of several family trips in my early childhood. It was more gorgeous than ever, covered with fresh snow, and bringing back fond memories. I stayed at the lookout for quite a while. For a moment, I felt my father's arms around me again. I closed my eyes and thanked God for precious parents and a beautiful childhood.

All in all, it was a good start of a new year within which was hidden new adventures to new places.

Little did I realize that the carefree, pleasure-filled time started me on a road which was not in the will of my Maker. It was a savory way to slide away from Him, and I did not feel like thinking about it. I felt that it would have spoiled the fun.

36

Tom

January 1957

Vienna, Austria to Halifax, Canada

Emigrating

En Route to the Harbor

FINALLY, THE date arrived for us to depart for Canada. As the train pulled out of Vienna, I felt nostalgia for the city which had treated us so well. The sounds, the lights, the smiles, and the vigor had been a refreshing experience.

The train was loaded primarily with Hungarian refugees heading for Ostende, the significant seaport of Belgium. Everybody was talking about Vienna, the Austrians, and the Western atmosphere. We all had to conclude that the step we had made when we left Hungary appeared to have been worth the risk. We were filled with anticipation.

We enjoyed the ride thoroughly, drinking in the scene of lands we had not been allowed to visit. We talked about our plans, where we planned to go, and why. Many of us had no idea which Canadian city to choose, but we had to decide. The choices were entered next to our name in the logbook of a Hungarian-Canadian pastor who acted as our guide on the journey.

Once the listing was completed, we were divided into groups, one would cross the Atlantic by airplane and others would cross by boat. John and I were assigned to the flight, but we exchanged our tickets for the boat. When else would we have the chance to cross the ocean by ship? Then we were sorted into which vessels we would take. It so happened that John was slated to travel on the HMS Empress of Britain, while I was to be ferried across by the HMS Saxonia. Both ships were waiting for us in Liverpool, England.

The trip to Ostende took about twelve hours with several stops, twice in the middle of the night. We were greeted everywhere by volunteers expressing their enthusiastic camaraderie and offering us free hot chocolate, cold drinks, and sandwiches. In Ostende, we boarded the ferry and crossed the English Channel in cold, foggy weather. The choppy waters soon affected the mood of many. Water-resistant paper bags were in high demand.

When my father had told us about his difficulty every time he crossed the Channel, I wondered why he could not conquer it by considering the simple fact that the ship had to roll with the waves. He had suggested that I put this into practice when I found myself in such a situation. Here was my chance to fight waves with logic. It worked.

I watched the shores of Europe fade into the distance and went to the front of the ship to see what was ahead. I was particularly interested in a first glimpse of the famed, white cliffs of Dover made so popular by poets, writers, and World War II movies. The four-hour journey lasted well into the evening, and to my regret, all I could see at the end were the lights of the city of Dover. The cliffs looked gray as we disembarked, but the thrill of stepping onto the soil of England was an event to remember.

England!

I was fond of the English. I had met only a very few, but had read many books, particularly during my Boy Scout years, and had developed an affection for their persistence, integrity, and dry sense of humor. I could hardly wait to meet some of the English and, hopefully, see a bit of their country.

The railway cars on which we had ridden to Ostende had been rolled onto the ferry and were now pulled out onto land. Soon we were on our way to Liverpool. As luck would have it, our whole trip was at night, and I could barely see anything in the darkness. Disappointed, I lay down and dozed to the sound of the clicking train wheels.

When I awoke in the morning, the train was motionless. We were in Liverpool, right at the dockside. I brushed my teeth, shaved, and opened the window. There, within thirty feet, I saw my first Englishman. He was mopping the floor and had a bucket ready for rinsing the mop. I greeted him, testing what I thought or hoped was my fluent English. He returned it with a kind but quiet hello.

. "How is life in Liverpool?" I asked. "As you can see we just arrived during the night."

"Fine, thanks," he answered. "Not much going on except that my boss kicked the bucket last night."

"Accidentally or was he just being rude?" I asked.

The man leaned on the mop, and his whole body shook with laughter.

"Young man, you are priceless!" he chuckled. "Don't you know what it means to kick the bucket?"

"Sir, I know what kick means, and I know what a bucket looks like, and I can see yours right here. What in the world makes you laugh?"

"Well, after someone 'kicks the bucket,' he does not kick anything anymore. He is put to rest in a wooden box we call a casket and, if he is lucky, a few close relatives and friends remember his name for a year or two. My boss died yesterday, young man. Sorry for using an expression you were not familiar with. Farewell to you now and good luck in Canada. I hear it is a nice country with lots of room and less rain that we are blessed with here in good, old England."

With this, he walked away carrying the mop and the bucket as well as my pride. Nevertheless, I learned a new English expression, soon to be followed by many more.

Within a half hour, activity on the train became very alive. Buses took us to a center nearby where we were treated to an English breakfast of eggs and sausages. The latter may have been the best but tasted strange to my Hungarian stomach. I gulped down some good tea and at least felt no hunger for a few hours.

We had fun as we rode on the double-decker bus on the left-hand side of the road watching the famous "bobbies." Strange price tags in shop windows caught our eye – three numbers separated by two slashes.

Grabbing our belongings, we followed an immigration official to the impressive HMS Saxonia. As we passed the purser's office, we received our boarding passes, which indicated our assigned cabin numbers.

The ship was beautiful. One can feel the immensity of an ocean liner only when one is near or inside one. They are masterpieces and things of beauty. We passed through long corridors, lounge rooms, and open halls, and settled into our small cabins with anticipation. It was good to get refreshed in the bathroom after two days of travel, and I prepared for a quick nap before exploring the ship. A knock on the door woke me up.

The Rabbi's Toothache

Apparently, my name was listed as one who spoke fluent English. A junior purser had come to ask me to assist them. An old rabbi among us had developed an acute toothache. The ship's chief purser thought it would be a good idea to relieve him of this problem while we were still docked, even at the expense of some delay in the departure.

We took a cab to the dentist's office with the old man who looked like a patriarch with his big, six-foot-four frame and a beard. The boat official piloted the taxi driver to the office with skill; this was obviously not the first time he had had to perform this task. In a few minutes, the rabbi was sitting in the dentist's chair, and the doctor asked me to interpret his assessment of the situation.

The size of the rabbi's teeth matched the size of the man. Saving the tooth causing the trouble was not an option, and it would take some work to extract.

"Don't tell him, Mr. Gerendas, but he has teeth and bones like a bull. It will be a tough job."

While he probably understood nothing that was said, the rabbi sensed the essence of the message.

"Just tell the doctor to take his time and do as he pleases. I have gone through enough in my life, he does not have to be overly gentle with me."

What followed was quite an experience. I decided to watch the effort in every detail, partly to test my own emotional resistance to a surgery. With the skill of the dentist and the discipline of the old man, it all went well without a word of complaint.

When the operation was complete, we took a cab back to the ship, but this time, at my request, we took a little detour to give me a chance to see a bit of Liverpool while the ship was waiting for us. The Cunard official was a sport and proved to be an excellent tour guide. Our trip back took about forty minutes, compared to the ten-minute ride on our way to the office.

I thanked the official for the trip. He was pleased to do me the favor. The rabbi boarded the ship, the only sign of his ordeal being his half-numbed face. The engines were humming when we arrived, and within fifteen minutes, the HMS Saxonia pulled away from the shore.

It was strange to imagine that we would not see land for an entire week, but the whole journey was really the fulfillment of a dream. I stood at the stern and watched the shore fade into the distance amidst the shrieking of the seagulls following the ship.

Farewell, England! Farewell, Europe!

Across the Atlantic

After a little rest, I ventured out to explore the beautiful 26,000-ton ocean liner. What a ship! Five dining rooms, several bars, game rooms with ping-pong tables, a bowling alley, squash court, library, several movie theatres, chapels, exercise rooms, dance floors, and medical facilities – a floating city. No chance for boredom! I looked forward to the trip as we left land behind.

Following a snack, the purser asked me to join him for a cup of coffee. He hoped I would be available to help his crew communicate with the sizeable Hungarian contingent on the boat. This included accompanying the doctor on his rounds and in his office, translating the menus, assisting the waiters when taking orders, translating safety instructions, and a variety of other tasks.

This sounded like fun with a purpose! It would entail meeting members of the crew and my fellow refugees and learning the procedures on a big ship as it covered thousands of miles day and night in various weather conditions. I enjoyed the thought of becoming, in a sense, a part of the crew.

The food was delicious, and the dining experience was truly hilarious. Of the 500 or so Hungarians, very few spoke English and even those who did could hardly understand the menu. Chicken was ordered with two arms and fluttering hands, beef with the sound of a cow, and ice cream was ordered by licking an imaginary ice cream cone. Laughter filled the dining room during the ordering of every meal. Waiters coped with the problem cheerfully but looked drained after lunch was over. I was supposed to relieve them from this stress. I could see the importance of translating the menu.

This turned out to be a delightful exercise in both English and in culinary pleasures. Whenever I did not understand an item, I had an opportunity to taste it. This was no small treat after many lean years in Hungary and certainly no overeating during the process of emigration. The tastier the item appeared on the menu, the more I "needed" to taste it, often eliminating my need for the meal itself by the time I had translated the menu.

I also took the liberty of paraphrasing some of the words. I knew that Hungarians do not like lamb so "roasted lamb" was translated as "inedible lamb," "eggplant" as "pureed green sawdust." I also added footnotes and comments to make the menu a little more interesting. Little wonder the Hungarians were delighted with the new service. They laughed aloud at the expressions knowing well the character of the author and the innocence of the English staff who typed and distributed it without second-guessing its accuracy. My first literary effort was quite rewarding.

One day, the purser asked me why people were laughing as they read the menu. I asked him in return, "Would you not rejoice if you finally understood what to order? The people are happy with the service, happiness breeds jokes, and jokes result in laughter." He walked away scratching his head, and I had a strange feeling on my conscience.

Seasickness

Following lunch, we participated in an emergency drill to learn procedures for embarking onto and surviving in lifeboats. By this time, we were far from shore, and the mood of the Atlantic was getting unfriendly. Widespread seasickness left plenty of empty seats in the dining room at meal times.

The farther the ship proceeded, the larger the waves became. Our mattresses contracted and expanded under our weight all night as the ship went up and down. Whenever the bow hit the water, it felt as if the ship would crack. Eventually, ropes were hung in all the corridors and rooms for us to hold onto as we tried to walk from one place to another. Large items such as tables and chairs were tied to hooks to prevent the furniture from catapulting across the room. Dancers found themselves in alternate corners of the dance floor, sliding and screaming and thoroughly enjoying themselves.

The need for my services arose again as seasickness reached epidemic proportions. The doctor needed a translator as he responded to the many calls and made his rounds in what had become a floating, rocking and rolling hospital. While some passengers were just pale, weak, and nauseated, others were almost frantic, asking for a "mercy shot" to end it all. The ones who suffered the most were those who had stopped eating and had stopped moving around, choosing to lie in their stuffy rooms. Adding random motion such as walking, to the systematic, endless motion of the boat reduced its effect on one's system.

I was so busy with the doctor that I had no time to be seasick. Only once on the open deck on a sunny morning did I get into a little trouble. It was shortly after breakfast.

Some of the sick had managed to get dressed, put on their winter coats, and were sitting enjoying the sun and fresh sea air.

"Tom, still no seasickness?" one of them asked with good-natured envy.

"Not yet, pal," I said, "but if I think of those raw-tasting English sausages in Liverpool..."

I could not finish the sentence. My breakfast left me in one coherent stream over the rail, to the delight of the seagulls who were still with us, feeding on the trash thrown overboard several times a day.

As we approached waters about two days from Newfoundland, near where the Titanic sank in 1912, the sea got so rough that the ship had to stop for a day. Gales were whipping the ocean, and miniature icebergs were floating all around us.

At this point, the motion was so violent that all group entertainment was stopped. Out of 800 passengers, fewer than eighty showed up at meals. While there was no panic, there was some apprehension and concern, and there was an unsavory odor despite the wide application of air fresheners. Large as the ship had appeared at the dockside in Liverpool, it seemed to be very small and fragile now that we were out at sea surrounded by fifty-foot waves and roaring winds.

The next day, the captain decided to proceed, and to the joy of all, the peg indicating our position on the map was moved another inch toward Canada. This map was displayed near the purser's office and was the source of hope to all who battled seasickness.

Land!

Just as we had become accustomed to living on the floating hotel, which was by this time slicing through less violent waters, the announcement came that the next day we would reach the Canadian shore.

The news electrified the atmosphere. Suddenly, it dawned on us that our life together was coming to an end. In a sense, it appeared that after a short, transient period, we were at the doorstep of another life. Even though the land was hidden from us, we trusted the captain's announcement and arranged our last day in light of the assurance of leaving the ship soon.

Of course, we had known, or at least firmly hoped, that the day would come when we would see the other side. But it felt so distant that we eventually had settled into a lifestyle as if it would last forever. Yet when the news about the forthcoming arrival came, suddenly we changed our regular routines, rearranged our suitcases for land travel, and made friends with many who we may not previously have engaged in conversation, jotting down future addresses.

Instead of sitting in the lounge, we suddenly had the urge to stroll on the deck or sit at a window facing the bow. Our thoughts, priorities, and eyes were fixed on the horizon ahead.

There will be a day in the life of all of us when we will approach the shores of the "other side." Preparing ourselves for the transition and becoming familiar with its terms and conditions, we can then enjoy and use the present journey more intelligently and with realistic anticipation.

By late afternoon, just about everyone was packed and ready for the transition to land. As we searched the horizon, every cloud appeared as a mountain, and whenever it separated from the water, it turned into another false hope. Soon the stars appeared and darkness settled around us. The water was calm – quite a contrast to the storm of several days before.

Then, in the distance right above the water, we spotted a faint light. There was no way to tell whether it was the light of another ship or the first light on the land. A few minutes later we spotted five or six lights far apart.

"Shore!"

All of the passengers joined us in the simple but very meaningful spectacle. About a quarter of an hour later it appeared as if thousands of little stars had settled on the horizon. It was an unforgettable sight. There in the distance was the New World – Canada – the land we had the privilege to choose as our next home.

The closer we got, the more abundant the lights became. It was strange to realize that, for the first time in our lives, we were approaching another world, where people were having supper, cars were stopping at traffic lights designed and manufactured there, and patients were being cared for in hospitals – all the result of a culture which had started there just a few hundred years ago.

This may sound trivial to the traveler who crosses the ocean in six hours by plane several times a year. But if you spend eight full days approaching the other side for the first time in your life, the distance seems enormous, and the existence of another culture in a land so far away is fascinating.

By now, the water was completely calm, and we saw clearly the outline of an oil refinery with its many lights and its torch fueled by gases leaving the chimneys, as well as the lights of thousands of illuminated windows. Soon we could see moving lights hugging the surface – cars scurrying along the shore.

The ship, which appeared so much smaller when it was tossed in the storm in the middle of the mighty Atlantic, once again looked majestic as it floated into the harbor of Halifax, Nova Scotia.

I could not stop drinking in every detail. The shape of the houses, the cars, buses, forklifts, and the people working at the dockside.

Tom – January 1957

As the propellers were reversed, the ship slowed down and, with perfect accuracy, slipped alongside the dock. The ropes were tied down, and with that the journey across the Atlantic was over.

37

Tom

1957-1960

Canada

First Steps in the New World

IT TOOK an hour or two to pass through immigration. Canadian volunteers welcomed us with warm smiles and an abundance of sandwiches, soup, and hot and cold drinks. The news of our fight and plight had crossed the ocean, and this first encounter with Canadians gave us good hopes of being accepted and treated well. Many chose Halifax as their new home. The rest of us boarded the train going west.

The trip to Toronto took a day and a half. The seats folded down into beds so I had a reasonable rest. As we sped along the snowy countryside, I was surprised at what I saw – houses made of wood and telephone and electrical cables strung on poles, even in cities. In Hungary, cables were always underground. This seeming backwardness was different from what I had expected.

I had a chance to read the Montreal Star newspaper on the train and was delighted to notice an advertisement enticing young people to join the armed services. After the state-dictated life where everything was compulsory, this was like a breath of fresh air.

We arrived in Toronto in the late afternoon. Buses took us through slushy, smoky sections of the city to the local headquarters of the Salvation Army. We were treated to a light lunch and an opportunity to pick any item of clothing we desired. While the clothing was not new, it was clean and of much better quality than what we were used to. It had been a long time since I looked like a gentleman and was warm on a cold day. It felt really good! While far away from a daily walk with God, I was grateful for His providence through this wonderful organization, which puts faith into action.

For decades after this experience, I recounted to Salvation Army people and Christmastime bell-ringers how they clothed me at a time when I had nothing, except what I had on my back and in my briefcase, before handing them my donation.

My first impression of Toronto was quite depressing. Under the skyscrapers, we saw gloomy streets, billboards, disorderly shops with handwritten "sale" signs, cars in poor repair, the ever-present above-ground electrical cable poles, and old-fashioned streetcars – a far cry from the pictures in the magazines advertising this great country.

Our destination was 5000 Queen Street West, an old building which had been converted into an immigration camp. The camp was in the district of used car lots decorated with strings of glaring and blinking light bulbs. I had a brief walk after supper and, when I returned to my bunk bed, I was awake for hours wondering if I had made the right choice when I traded beautiful Vienna for what this place seemed to be. It was certainly my first depressing experience since I had left Hungary and my first acquaintance with some of the dismal realities of North American cities.

Finding a Job

I arrived in Canada with twelve dollars in my pocket. Fortunately, my needs were in line with my budget. We were fed and had free lodging for a few weeks until we found a job. The job hunting was made easier by volunteers who dispatched us to places where there were openings. Streetcar tickets were our only real expense, and they were a mere ten cents.

Consequently, with the twelve dollars in my pocket, I felt financially secure – in fact, too secure. When I lost my fountain pen, I purchased a Mont Blanc for nine dollars. The three dollars I had left would keep me going for at least two weeks, and I was not concerned about problems further away.

Looking back, having nothing simplified my life greatly. I was free from the many distractions caused by having to deal with things I owned.

I was quite certain that I would get a job soon. Knowing the language and having a good engineering diploma, I did not expect any difficulty. However, the first job openings I investigated were ones for which the employers considered me overqualified. I applied for a job to unload bread trucks at night but was not trusted to stick around for any length of time before landing a better job. Each night, I returned to find fewer and fewer of the twenty beds occupied, and I was the guy who was fluent in English and had an engineering degree. I started to get concerned.

It looked advisable to reopen my contact with God and ask for a little assistance. It was strange to pray after not having given Him any thought for several weeks. Even though I lacked the assurance of friendship with Him, I hoped He would respond to my sincere repentance as I prayed.

Within a week, I had three offers: one from Ontario-Hydro, the elite hydroelectric power operation; one from Canadian National Railways; and the third from Canadian General Electric Company.

The Ontario-Hydro job sounded fascinating and my experience was applicable. Mechanical surface stress measurements were one of my specialties. This job would involve electric strain gauges, and I was to work for an engineering executive who was delighted to find someone who had practical experience with this new technology.

However, the man in Personnel, even though an immigrant himself, thought that the job was too advanced for someone "just off the boat." He offered me a beginner's training course. My prospective boss was disappointed, and I left the Personnel Manager standing there as I folded my briefcase without saying a word and left.

The railway job was also closely related to my background, but in the government-operated office, everyone appeared so sleepy and position-conscious, I was sure to be frustrated.

Canadian General Electric

I was quite impressed by the preliminary interview at Canadian General Electric (CGE) and was asked by the Director of Engineering Personnel to report to the Peterborough headquarters for a more specific evaluation. I had run out of money and was not in a position to buy a train ticket to Peterborough, Ontario. At that moment, a vice president who frequently commuted to the office in Peterborough, walked by. When he was informed about my situation and my recent escape from Hungary, he said he would gladly offer me round-trip transportation on his next weekly commute.

The trip with this fine gentleman was my introduction to the ethical, humane, executive type about whom one seldom reads in the papers. The warmth of his personality, his wisdom, and sense of humor came when I needed it most. Along the way to Peterborough, we stopped for coffee during which he asked me to elaborate on life under Communism and my experiences during the escape.

Once we arrived at the large plant, he took me to my interviewer and advised him of where he could be reached in order to meet for our ride back. I sensed respect from all who saw me under his wing.

The interview was promising and the atmosphere vibrant. The job would involve working at four different plants within the first year as a member of a test course. It would allow me to get a feel for the company and give the company a feel for my abilities. This opportunity would offer challenge, variety, and a chance to live in four different places – just what my tourist spirit needed. Of the three options I was evaluating, the pay would be the lowest but the learning potential would be the highest.

I used the drive back to Toronto to pick the vice president's brain about the options. He was most helpful in looking at the choices from all angles but hoped I would choose CGE if they extended an offer. I appreciated his kindness and candor.

The offer was extended to me the following day, and I accepted without hesitation.

Guelph, Ontario

That Saturday, I packed my few belongings and went to the railway station by public transportation deciding to save the money designated for the taxi. At the station, I indulged in a pretzel to add flavor to the short train ride, a pleasant break after weeks of city life in Toronto.

I was met by an immigration official whose job was to find housing and keep an eye on new immigrants until they got established. The tall, lean man drove me across town to the home of an Austrian couple and gave me his card. "Call me if you need more help. If you stay out of trouble, you will enjoy your hosts. They have helped a good number of young fellows and girls in their first steps in Canada."

The Posch Family

To my pleasant surprise, the family had come to Canada from Vienna, my new favorite city. Almost instantly, we began to converse in German. I soon found myself at the lunch table of a friendly family which included several young adults who either boarded in their home or belonged to their large circle of friends.

Later, more friends dropped in, mostly Canadians but some from other countries. I felt instantly at home, and by the end of the day, I felt like I had a lot more than just food and shelter. In my mind, eleven dollars a week for room and board and good company was a pretty good deal. With a starting salary of $375 per month and no real needs to speak of, I was sure to do well.

Sunday morning was bright and beautiful. My room overlooked a small square in a pleasant, well-kept neighborhood where people took pride in manicuring their lawns. I stood at the window watching people walk by the funeral home across the street on their way to church. The owner stood at the sidewalk shaking hands with his future clients. I wondered if this handshake helped him to do his forecast.

Following breakfast, we drove to the Posch's church, where the service was good and the fellowship was warm. Sunday afternoon was open house again. It took me a few days to realize that the Posch home was a continuous open house. I still wonder how Walter, a mechanic, was able to finance the continuous parties. Somehow the table was always well-supplied with great European food.

On Monday, I reported to work. The plant was on the way to Walter's workplace, so he gave me a ride every morning. The city bus brought me home every night. The job was interesting, and the fellow test engineers were bright and funny, but it took me a few weeks to feel I was part of the group. It helped to play chess, a fad during lunch introduced by a German technician who greatly helped me to adjust to this new experience.

The great moment came on Friday when I pocketed my first paycheck: SEVENTY DOLLARS! It was an incredible feeling to be rich – instantly. I paid off my rent and the ten dollars Walter had loaned me, put forty dollars in the bank, and loaded my wallet with ten dollars of spending money.

I worked overtime and quickly accumulated some wealth. I had no need of a car, entertainment was free, and my hostess packed my lunchbox, so my only indulgence was an occasional soft drink for a dime. My weekly deposits increased at a good clip.

Peterborough and the Hendersons

Guelph was followed by Peterborough, Ontario, the switchgear operation of CGE near beautiful Kawartha Lake. I had found out from the boys in the plant that Peterborough was a great place for summer fun, so I had expressed a "genuine" interest in testing switchgear when I was interviewed for the next assignment.

On a bright Saturday morning, I said farewell and took off for Peterborough by train. It was a happy trip after a good experience, and I was looking forward to the next one. I settled into a hotel in Peterborough, and after a shower, began to check out the homes where previous GE test men had had a good boarding experience.

I was determined to look at all of the eleven homes listed before making a decision. Some were no longer interested in renting a room. Others were less to my liking. I hoped that the last one would be a viable solution. When I rang the bell on Sunday afternoon at the last house,

George Henderson opened the door with after-nap mist in his eyes.

"I am sorry to tell you that we have decided not to rent a room this summer," he said after I explained the reason for the visit. "However, I detect an accent and wonder where you are from?" he continued, more awake. When he found out that I was a very recent newcomer from Hungary, he had me sit down for a cup of tea and to meet his wife.

Jean Henderson entered with a charming smile and placed a cup of tea and a few cookies on the table. After a brief chat they looked at each other and said, "Why don't we take Tom?"

George insisted that I check out of the hotel immediately and move in early enough so we could go fishing in the evening. One hour later, George and I were on our way to a pond north of Peterborough with his fishing gear and a thermos full of hot tea. All my belongings stayed spread out in the room waiting to be organized.

We caught nothing but had a good time. When we got home, around 1:00 a.m., George wanted me to taste his sandwich specialty: grilled steak with a variety of flavors added to it. That was followed by another cup of tea and a relaxed chat. By 3 a.m., I was in bed – well prepared to report to my new job at 7 a.m.!

A few hours later, I staggered into the dining room half asleep and quickly ate the breakfast Jean had prepared for me. I was well into my fifteen-minute walk to the CGE plant before I was fully awake.

Cars in Hungary?

Frank Thompson, an Englishman in our group, asked me if we had cars in Hungary. I informed him horses were the preferred mode of transport by Hungarians, that we rode our horses to stores, hitched them to hitching posts, and in this fashion, we got around.

Ten minutes later at coffee break, I heard a roar of laughter. Frank apparently had passed on his new-found information regarding the Hungarian method of transportation. They were aware from prior conversations with me that not only had Hungary had cars since the late 1880s, but we had the first electric subway in Europe in 1896.

Frank did not talk to me for days.

We became friends again after I had saved $813 for the purchase of my first car, a beautiful, shiny, blue and white 1952 Pontiac. Frank liked to travel, and the "Blue Beauty" provided him with transportation. He taught me how to drive, and we and two other guys enjoyed traveling to the north and south on weekends.

One of these trips led us to nearby Kawartha Lakes. Deciding to teach ourselves to water ski, we rented a motorboat and skis and cast lots to determine who would go first. After each of us was dragged off the dockside a bit early, we all mastered the sport and, afterwards, celebrated at a cheerful pub.

Heading to Montreal

The CGE Personnel Supervisor appeared again, and we decided that the General Electric Major Appliance Works in Montreal would be a good next stop for me.

It goes without saying that the tourist in me was again a major factor in this decision. Following twenty-four years of restricted mobility behind the Iron Curtain, my primary interest was to see new places and faces, and colorful Montreal with its French and European flavor attracted me.

As I pulled out of the Henderson's driveway, it felt once again like I was leaving home. But nostalgia turned to excitement at the prospect of a new place with new experiences.

Settling in Montreal

During the five-hour drive from Peterborough to Montreal, I had the chance to reflect on the rich events of the last six months and tried to imagine what life would be like in Montreal, a world class city of beauty and vibrant activity with a French flavor.

As I noticed the lights of the big city in the distance, my heart began to beat a bit faster. I knew that this would be a very different environment after solid, calm, English-Canadian Peterborough. I was still a new driver, and soon found myself in the middle of honking horns, screeching brakes, cars switching lanes, and passing on both the left and the right. I counted myself fortunate to be alive when I pulled into a motel to set up my temporary headquarters. The next two days were occupied with searching through "Room To Let" ads and checking out one after the other. I found a very attractive room for ten dollars per week at a home about six minutes away from the GE plant.

The Beaulieu's home was spotless, bright, and well-furnished. Mr. and Mrs. Beaulieu lived with Mrs. Beaulieu's sister. The two ladies of the home had all the time in the world to keep it neat. They allowed me to use a small refrigerator, a double hot plate, and a few shelves in the basement for preparing my breakfasts and dinners. It was a perfect place for living and for a chance to polish my French.

The Beaulieus kept everything so immaculate that I was not even allowed to wash my car in the driveway, but I could not see spending two to three dollars at a car wash. Instead, I bought a rope and a bucket and made it a routine to drive down to the St. Lawrence River on Saturday mornings to wash the Blue Beauty.

The riverbank was a favorite early morning strolling place for a few priests in the area. We developed a relationship, and we became a team as I washed the car. Two or three priests wiped and polished, adding upper body exercise to their walking routine. It was a great way to get the job done and have a good time. The French-speaking Fathers would switch to English out of courtesy, which I returned with hot coffee served from my Thermos bottle.

Job

The job at the GE plant was a totally new field for me: household refrigerator testing and development. I was led into this effort by Pat, a delightful, competent engineer, the six-foot-four son of a Saskatchewan farmer. Pat was a great guy to work for. He had a good sense of humor and, partly due to pressure from his boss, was a tough taskmaster. In order to get up to speed more quickly, on many an occasion I would start in the morning, work through the night – taking a nap on bubble wrap in the test lab – and leave the next evening after thirty-six hours on the job.

My next assignment would have been in the instruments division of GE in Quebec City. I was anxious to live a few months in this beautiful, historic, very French place with the most European atmosphere on the continent. I had visited it twice with friends and liked it more each time, but just before the test course personnel official would have called to confirm my transfer, my manager called me into his office.

"Tom, we like the way you operate. I am ready to offer you a permanent job if you are interested."

"I really appreciate this, Francis. I like it here, too, but please hold the job for me until I have a chance to do the Quebec assignment. As you know, I am still savoring being able to see new places after a decade of having been locked up in Hungary. Quebec looks like so much fun!"

"Tom, do me a favor. Discuss this opportunity with your compatriots and tell them you can have a job here and now. With the current economic uncertainty, it may or may not be available three months from now."

I did what he suggested, and everyone I consulted was wondering how I could even think about gambling with the job just to have another tourist opportunity. I signed up and, sure enough, the clouds on the economic scene became darker every week. At the end of the test course year, only twelve of the 122 test men were offered employment.

I enjoyed the fullness of the task. It was theory, experiment, development, and production engineering all rolled into one. It gave me an opportunity to work with almost everyone in the 800-person plant.

My French became very useful, particularly on the production floor. When the French-Canadian assemblers noticed that I began by speaking with them in French, they switched to English to make it easier for me. It was only a short time before I began to feel part of the team. They were a hard-working, good-natured group, and quite cosmopolitan.

A crucial part of my job was figuring out why refrigeration systems would fail as they made their way down the assembly line. Time was of the essence because for every hour that the line was not in operation there was a serious impact on the paychecks of the assemblers. I had to rely on my judgment and well-organized data to avoid lengthy shutdowns. It was a great way to gain appreciation from both assemblers and the management.

The way the company was run was great training for a young professional. We felt the power and resources of the giant company behind us, yet had the flexibility and efficiency of the smaller organization. They made us, the engineers, feel part of the management, providing courses and arranging meetings for our professional development.

At one of the meetings, we were asked if we had any ideas for improving the products. I suggested we modify the front door of the high-end refrigerators so that customers could access ice cold water and ice cubes from the outside, without having to open the door. The discussion leader thought it was a good idea, but wondered if customers would be willing to shell out eighty dollars for such a feature. Nevertheless, he promised he would pass the idea on to the marketing department for evaluation.

I received a commendation for creativity, but it was felt that customers would balk at the higher pricing for this feature. This was in 1959, and it wasn't more than a decade before refrigerators were available with this feature.

I loved my job and felt I could remain working there until I retired.

Adrift

I felt myself slipping further and further away from God as I tried to make myself comfortable at places where I could find instant satisfaction. It started with YMCA dances and ended at shady nightclubs. I knew something was wrong. There was a split in my life which did not allow me to find peace.

I began sampling churches on Sundays to renew my contact with fellow Christians. I liked the small Cote des Neiges Presbyterian Church, where a young elder named Derek reached out to me. He was a strong believer with a good Irish sense of humor. Derek invited me over for meals and accepted me as I was, without ever judging me. He did not realize what those simple dinners meant to me.

My other contact was Mrs. Gordon, a godly and sharp woman in her seventies. She had been "dispatched" by a retired minister with whom I had corresponded for years and visited in Philadelphia on vacation. He had realized I was on loose terms with God and asked Mrs. Gordon to keep an eye on me. She invited me for a modest but very nice dinner on the first Friday of each month. God used her and Derek to show His continued determination to not let me drift further away from Him.

Mother Sets Sail

I kept in touch with Mother mainly by phone, which by now I could afford. She was doing well but hoped to join me one day.

I was ready to have her join me after a year and a half of being on the loose. I knew she would not be pleased with my recently evolved lifestyle, but neither was I. Her godliness would provide stability and be a beneficial influence. Her positive attitude promised that I would enjoy the opportunity to return a fraction of her sacrificial love towards me for the twenty-five years of my life.

It was easy for her to get permission to leave Hungary. By letting her leave, the government would have one less pensioner for whom they would be obligated to provide. A long list of Communists waited for an apartment to become available, and there were plenty of folks who were happy to take over her tobacco store.

She received her papers for departure in three months. I arranged for her train and boat tickets, found a nice, two-bedroom apartment in the cosmopolitan area of Cote des Neiges and filled it with simple but attractive furniture. It was within walking distance of Cote des Neiges Presbyterian Church, which I thought she might like to attend. I had no questions about the members welcoming her warmly.

Mother Arrives

It was a wonderful day when I saw her waving to me from the boat as it docked in Montreal harbor. There was a flood of tears, great joy, and warm hugs when she stepped on the shore. We were united again and right there said a prayer of gratitude to the One who helped make it happen.

She was surrounded in minutes by friends she had made during the journey across the Atlantic, mainly young women in their twenties who had shared their life stories and wanted to make sure they would be able to keep calling her after they settled in Canada.

She looked rested and very well at age fifty-three. Apparently, she had won the couples' dance contest on the boat with a gentleman from Scotland who was graciously loaned to her by his wife who was in a wheelchair. The crossing had been in good weather and calm seas, and she had enjoyed every minute.

We found and loaded her luggage into my car and headed for a cup of coffee in Old Montreal. She thoroughly enjoyed our half-hour sightseeing tour that ended at the top of Westmount, where she admired the sea of lights and enjoyed the balmy breeze. We leaned over the railing and chatted for a good while before driving home. After a light dinner, we unpacked her things, beginning her stay with me in a home she really liked.

She adjusted to her new life without any problems. Her outgoing personality, lack of inhibition when speaking English despite a strong Hungarian accent, and sincere faith gained her acceptance everywhere. In fact, her creative expressions in English were a source of good-natured laughter wherever she went.

She found a job wrapping presents at Simpson's Department Store. Through an agency, she also frequently babysat, often in very elegant homes. The children loved and respected her, and their mothers sought her advice about many things, including their fashion decisions. Being someone who spoke her mind, she told them in no uncertain terms when she thought a dress did not enhance their appearance. Both activities helped her gain confidence and some financial independence. Her Hungarian friends helped her feel even more at home. Her delicious meals, her care for the household and apartment, and her morale were a joy for me.

Mother found more difficult to accept my lifestyle than to adjust to her new environment. With patience and understanding, she reminded me of my need to return to a walk of faith. Try as I might, I was unable to convince her that this was only a temporary detour from the path I intended to follow.

Truthfully, I had difficulty convincing myself. I had a lot of fun socially – trips, tennis, swimming, skiing, concerts, and other events filled my time, but my heart was not at peace. I began wondering if there was a way to have fun and peace simultaneously.

38

Tom

1960

Montreal, Canada

Good Move

THAT YEAR, 1960, turned out to be my last with CGE. The company was having a particularly tough time – projects abounded, but we were understaffed. It was not unusual for me to work twenty to thirty-six hours at a time in order to resolve problems which threatened to shut down the assembly line.

It was a rewarding but extremely tiring experience. My boss and I could hardly wait for vacation to rescue us. We were at the end of our rope and ready for a real rest. We embraced each other on the last day of work.

I was becoming increasingly aware of how far I had let myself slide away from God. Being overworked made me realize that something was missing in my life, something that I had experienced in the past – the closeness of my heavenly Father. I knew that He still loved me, but I felt like the prodigal son. It was hard to pray with the same ease as I had when I felt closer to Him. I began to pray with the guilt and hesitation of an unfaithful friend trying to renew a tarnished relationship.

I decided to look for a place to vacation where I could enjoy my favorite sports, but where I could also find the company of Christian young adults, hopefully including some nice girls who were trying to live in harmony with God. I asked Mrs. Gordon for a recommendation during one of our Friday dinners.

She suggested a camp called "Word of Life," located on beautiful Schroon Lake in the Adirondack Mountains, a three-hour drive from Montreal. To make sure that it was the right spot, I drove down one weekend to check it out.

The place was beautifully kept. There were opportunities for swimming, boating, water skiing, tennis, and most importantly, plenty of young people having fun. The place radiated what I was longing for – a cheerful Christian atmosphere. I put down a deposit and drove home knowing that I had made the right step.

I could hardly wait for the day when I could start my vacation. I did a little shopping to refresh my wardrobe just in case I met a young lady to my liking. I also polished my 1957 Chevrolet convertible, which I had purchased to facilitate my agenda.

Mother was delighted by the prospect of me spending a week in a Christian atmosphere. I found out later that she and Mrs. Gordon were on their knees every day during my vacation praying for God to touch my heart and for me to yield to His call.

Tom – 1960

New Direction

The weather was gorgeous on the day I was off to Word of Life Camp. I drove away in my new convertible with the top down, good music playing, wearing classy sunglasses, feeling like a million dollars, and all set for a great week of physical and spiritual refreshment.

I arrived in the early afternoon. The place was like a beehive. Groups of folks were saying farewells and exchanging addresses while we new arrivals registered and got settled in our rooms. After that, we had a fancy dinner, followed by orientation and a light-hearted evening of singing and worship.

The food was excellent, the service superb, and volleyball, tennis, swimming, and evening entertainment made each day fun and interesting. At dinner, we had the opportunity to get dressed up and feel a bit more dignified.

One night, I joined my table a little late after a quick trip to the bait and tackle store nearby to get plastic worms for some early morning fishing. After taking my seat, my undisciplined eyes spotted the deep cut on the back of the blouse of a cute girl at the next table, just within arm's reach. I wondered how she would react if I dipped one of my plastic worms into the cold ice water in my glass and slipped it down her back.

She let out an ear-shattering shriek and turned around at lightning speed to find the culprit. Without any investigation, she yelled at me – one out of eight at our table!

"You are the only rascal who could have thought of such beastly mischief!" The other guests were shocked at first but recovered quickly, and peace returned to the dining room.

By the end of dinner, my victim and I were friends again. She gave me a reconciling hug but kept the worm as a souvenir of her harrowing experience. She was a nice girl, and it was a very nice worm.

The daily morning Bible studies were conducted by Dr. Charles Woodbridge in a beautiful but modest chapel. Dr. Woodbridge was in his early sixties and was blessed with both a great sense of humor and an immense knowledge of the Bible. He became a favorite to our group. To us, he seemed to be a truly God-fearing man and a down-to-earth coach with obvious compassion.

As I sat on the chapel bench listening to him on the Wednesday morning, my thoughts began to wander. Here I was in the cheerful company of Christians where I felt I was surrounded by genuine joy in a wholesome atmosphere. I compared this to my inconsistent life where the gap between my Saturday nights and Sunday mornings was a mile wide. I was hanging on, but there was no security and no balance in my life. I felt empty, phony, and without character. For the first time, I despised the way I was wasting my life. I realized that it was as if I was back home in God's family where I belonged. A new-found peace settled in my heart. I realized that God was giving me another chance to walk with Him. I felt that if I went back into the lifestyle I had left in Montreal, I might play away the rest of my life.

I was so deep in my thoughts that I was unable to listen to the teaching and participate in singing. I decided to make a move. At the end of the Bible study hour, I approached Dr. Woodbridge and asked if he would be willing to spend a little time with me before the week was over.

"Why don't you come see me at my cottage after the Friday night service?" he asked.

I leapt at the invitation and looked forward to the session, which might straighten out my inconsistent life.

As Friday night approached, I became increasingly excited about the prospect of having a one-on-one session with Dr. Woodbridge.

We sat down in his cottage near the chapel, and he gently asked me to share my concerns. I realized all the years I had wasted as I went my own way and compared this to the week I had so enjoyed. I became overwhelmed and could not say anything for about two minutes.

When I regained control, I told him briefly how dissatisfied I was with my instability and fruitlessness as a Christian. I wanted to recommit my life to God. How should I go about it now that I really meant business?

I was ready for an in-depth analysis of my life and attitudes by this great servant of God. I wanted to go through a thorough, complex counseling "operation."

"Tom, do you start and end the day with some communication with God? I mean real, live communication, not a harried, brief ritual, but a deep quiet time of prayer and at least a brief but attentive study of His Word."

"No, Doc. I can't say I do this," I confessed.

"Tom," Dr. Woodbridge answered, "I have no further questions. You see, there is no way to walk with Him without regular communication with Him. We all are exposed to the influences and noises of the world, including the Evil One, all day long. That lifeline of quiet time at least exposes our soul to a moment of undisturbed relationship with God. It stills our heart and allows us to get perspective, and it allows God to reach us without us being distracted."

"O.K., Doc," I said. "I am ready to do this, but this alone cannot be the answer to my whole problem! I can see it is a great step forward, but my whole life is a scattered medley of experiences without a meaningful, structured purpose."

"Tom, you are looking for a complicated cure for a complicated problem. What you don't realize is that while your problem has truly become complicated, its cause is quite simple! You unplugged yourself from the power source! You cut yourself off from the two direct lines from God – undisturbed prayer and reading His Word with an attentive, listening heart. Frankly, I have never yet seen a consistently fruitful Christian at peace with God who did not make this simple practice his highest priority. Don't do it as an obligatory ritual, because it is not. Eating and drinking is not either, yet we all do it. Do it because your contact with God depends on it, and once you do it wholeheartedly, you will cherish it. I have told this to many Christians in your situation. They all looked for a complex cure for a major restructuring of their lives. Very few were willing to try this simple solution. Yet all who did told me that their lives changed, and all who did not, either kept on struggling or I never heard from them again. Give it a try! If you still need help, let me know. But please don't ask for my help if you are not willing to try it for at least a month or two because I will tell you the same thing, and we will both waste our time."

"I will try it, Doc," I said. And with that, our discussion was over. Dr. Woodbridge put his hand on my shoulder and prayed that God would help me stay close to Him and that I would try the daily time with Him.

I walked out of the cottage. It was a beautiful, starry summer night. The main building was full of life. The lights, sounds, and happy faces reflected the spirit of the last night. On Saturday, most people would leave and a new group of vacationers would arrive. Friday night was farewell night, time for fun and chatting in the snack area or for walks on the grounds.

The latter appealed to me, but something drew me to the porch of the cottage I was occupying. I opened my Bible to chapter one of Paul's letter to the Romans and started to read. I was anxious to start the experiment. The more I read, the more it came to life. I read it with a thirsty heart. I read it because I wanted to drink of the fountain of God-inspired blessing. While I had read these chapters often, this time I was reading them with the thirst of a seeking heart. It made all the difference.

As I drove home from World of Life Camp, I knew one thing. I was not going to experiment any more with God and with life. I was going to make one permanent adjustment – to wholly surrender to Him.

As I write these lines many decades later, I can attest to the fact that Dr. Woodbridge's simple advice truly did work. My morning quiet time before the hassle of each day began started me off on the right track. These times strengthened me when I was weak, humbled me when I was proud, enlightened me when I was confused, and calmed me when I was upset. It was more than just starting the day off right – it was a true heart-to-heart conversation with God.

It is so logical to start the day by connecting with God, similar to a briefing being most appropriate before the battle. Officers usually get their briefings at the start of the day, so that the day will be effective. At night, it is time for evaluation, reflection, repentance, and getting ready for rest.

There is another reason why spending time with God should be one of the first things we do in the morning. When we go to sleep, our mind, including our "directional gyroscope" gets powered down and dangles around while we are asleep. When we wake up, it gets powered up, which is the crucial time to let God set it to spin in the right direction.

Whenever I become slack in this practice, I see the negative effect on my life within days. I may have succeeded in many things during these periods, but there was little blessing or peace. Even though I may have failed in many things, during the regular quiet times with God, there was enlightenment and assurance.

Moving Forward

It was not going to be easy. I had strong relationships that could hold me to my old ways. They were with great people I respected, loved, and liked, but whose interests and lifestyle could not be reconciled with what I was now determined to pursue. I needed a new circle of friends who had similar desires. I particularly craved the companionship of a Christian woman who would be a partner in this effort and with whom I could have a relationship which would be acceptable to God.

When the time came to depart, I drove away, the top down, cruising under the starry sky. I prayed that God would help me go through this period of adjustment with His strength. Although I drove alone, the car slipping by beautiful countryside, I was not lonely. I felt God's presence so intensely that I kept talking to Him aloud, praising Him for this great experience which had brought a new perspective and a desire to follow Him.

Mrs. Gordon was visiting Mother when I arrived. They were delighted with the good news as well as with the visible effects of a sunny, sport-filled week. They confessed they had prayed daily for my week at the camp.

When these two prayed, they prayed with great faith. I have learned since that there is enormous power in the prayers of sincerely praying elderly ladies. When they get on their knees, the decibel meters in the heavenly receivers peg their needles! I believe, with my engineer's mind, that trusting prayers are the greatest intercessory power sources in existence. They can move mountains.

Back on Track

The first Sunday back at Cote des Neiges Church was so different! It followed the first week in years that my life had been consistent for seven days in a row including Saturday night. Singing hymns and reading the Bible was like drinking spring water out of a fountain. Fellowship with people, young and old, became so much more meaningful. Mother was delighted to see how I enjoyed being in church.

I joined the Young Peoples' Fellowship and the enjoyable Friday nights proved to be, not only compensation for what I had given up, but abundantly more. We had good discussions and Bible studies, listened to interesting speakers, went bowling, hiking, swimming, had cookouts, and helped each other as well as people outside the group.

I never missed my personal time with God and prayed daily to find a girl who would share my new perspective.

39

Jutta

Early September 1959

Germany to Canada

Across the Ocean

I BOOKED passage on the SS Maasdam to set sail in September.

I moved home for the two months before I was to leave. When Vati and Mutti asked me what I would like to do on my last day in Germany, I said I would like to have a boat ride on the Rhine. It was a special time, with lunch on the boat and a view of the Lorelai, a steep rock mountain on the east side of the river. There was a legend of a beautiful maiden who called to the boatmen, luring them to herself and making their boats crash on the rocks.

Vati and Mutti took the train with me from Bonn to Rotterdam. We had much to talk about looking back on our lives.

At the dock, Vati had tears in his eyes as he said, "Jutta, I don't think you will ever come back to live in Germany again."

I did not know what would have been the right answer, so I said nothing. I gave them another hug and boarded the ship.

I cried a little as the boat horn sounded its goodbye, and the ship's band played "Muss i' denn," a favorite

German folksong. I asked myself, "Did I go crazy to go to another country?"

Mutti and Vati told me later that their friends asked, "Are you crazy? You sent your twenty-three-year-old daughter on a boat? You don't know anything about the people on this boat!" My parent's friends were not wrong in warning them about a woman alone on such a ship. There were movies and dancing every night, and there were times that I did not feel safe.

There was a young Englishman among the passengers. He also was traveling alone. He must have noticed that I often sat by myself at the meals. I liked his British accent. He wanted to dance with me, but I said no, that I wanted to see the ship instead. I went to the bow where the captain sat. He was friendly and polite, but he told me that I was not allowed up there.

Another young man, who came with his whole family, called me and wanted to get together. I said I was busy. Another wanted to take me to a movie. I had to tell him to leave me alone.

There were four ladies sharing my cabin. Two were Jehovah's Witnesses. They presented their arguments for their faith. I was almost convinced, but there was something blocking the way to accepting their beliefs.

We were nine days on the ocean without seeing land in any direction. It was exciting when icebergs were spotted. We all rushed to the rail. The binoculars that the

Lehmanns had given me as a goodbye present were very popular.

Partway across the Atlantic, we ran into a storm. We heard that it was a strong hurricane that had moved up the east coast of America, and its center was now in the open ocean. I was seasick for the rest of the voyage.

On one of the worst days, when the steward put me onto my bed, I told him, "Listen, one more day and then I will jump over the railing." Lots of sharks followed our boat, because the crew threw all of our leftover food into the water. It was a wedding feast for the sharks. I had seen them, but it still seemed to be better than the seasickness. "Just throw me overboard."

I lay on my bed and ate only Saltine crackers to try to calm my stomach. It was the first time I had seen them. They helped, but did not make me feel better for long. (*Ever since then, when I see Saltines, I think of that voyage.)*

After a few days of the seasickness, the stewardess came and said, "Ms. Merkel, you have to have a bath. You cannot go on like this."

I sat in the tub, but I was not able to wash myself. The water was always where I was not. I chased the water for half an hour. I finally told the stewardess, "You have to ask the captain to make the ship stop moving back and forth." Our laughter helped me get through that time.

The Saint Lawrence River was relief from the storm and the seasickness. There were no waves for the two days as we sailed to Montreal. When I stepped ashore that morning, I thanked God that it was over and that we had arrived safely.

40
Jutta
Late September 1959-Spring 1961
Montreal, Canada

Life in the New World

BABETTE, MY FRIEND from the year in Lüneburg, had written to her sister, Marianne, that I was coming. I had met Marianne at Babette's wedding. She and her husband were waiting when the ship docked. They took me to their little apartment for the first few days in the country.

I had been told that the streets were paved with gold. I was quite disappointed to find that they were the same as those I had left in Germany.

I found a job as a governess for three children. Their father was a British lawyer and their mother was a doctor. Their home was a mansion in a good neighborhood. The family was "nose-in-the air" snobbish, and they made me feel like a maid.

The oldest son was about fifteen. He was always wanting to help me with the dishes in the kitchen and asking if he could set the table with me. I told him, "Du hast nicht alle Tassen im Schrank!" (literally, "You don't have all your cups in the cupboard!" or, "You're crazy.")

I was homesick. Every night, I heard horns blowing from ships in the river. I wished I was on that ship going home to Germany, but I did not have the money to consider it. In the mornings, my pillow was soaked from my tears.

I was terribly lonely. Marianne and her husband told me they did not want to see me as long as I was so sad about leaving Germany.

My parents could hear the desperation in my letters. Vati got in touch with the German embassy. One of their officials came to the house to check on me. It was wonderful to have someone take my side. I resigned shortly after his visit.

Mrs. McGillivary

I found a new position with an old Scottish lady, Mrs. McGillivray. I was to make her meals, read to her, and do other chores as she needed.

She was stingy. She always had lots of bananas. I had not seen bananas in years, and I wanted to eat five or six of them at once. One day, I ate one, and she shrieked in her high-pitched voice, "Who ate this banana?" When I said it was me, she responded, "Well, next time, ask me."

She wanted me to make her a shepherd's pie. No matter how many times I tried, I burned it. I talked back to her, "If you would buy a new oven, I would know how to do it." Her old rickety oven hardly worked any more. When her son was visiting, I asked him if he knew how to make it. He said, "Jutta, don't worry. She can live without shepherd's pie."

Mrs. McGillivray spoke fluent German. Every afternoon, I read aloud stories by the great German philosophers Schiller and Goethe.

I was not happy. I was lonely and desperate for a friend. I remembered the good fellowship I had with the Lehmanns and remembered their advice that I should look for a church. I thought now maybe I could talk to a pastor.

I was standing outside a church when a woman came up and asked if she could help. She heard a little of my story and invited me to come home with her. She was from Tunisia and her husband was from Germany. Both were devout Christians. Zena became like a sister to me.

Soon after I met Zena, she invited me to go skating with her and her friends. We had a wonderful time together. At one point, we were skating in a circle holding hands. Somehow, I lost my grip and landed on my right arm. At the hospital, we found out I had broken my elbow. They put it in a cast.

Back at Mrs. McGillivray's, I discovered that I couldn't take care of my long curly hair. I decided that the only way was to cut it off. I went to a hairdresser and told her I wanted short hair. She asked if I was sure about this. I said yes, but I cried as she cut it. In Germany, only people with a disease would have short hair. I tried to tell myself that it was different here in Canada.

Soon after that, I met Babette's brother, Peter von Sass. He worked in the mine fields in the north. Marianne arranged for us to meet. He was tall, blond, and good-looking, someone that some women would fall for, but I knew immediately that he was not the right one for me. I looked quite disheveled when I met him because I could not fix my hair with only one arm. He wrote a kind letter saying that we could not continue to date.

Mrs. McGillivray decided that with only one arm to use, I could not fulfill my duties for her, and she dismissed me.

Montreal General Hospital

Zena and her husband took me in while I looked for another position. I decided that I should look for a job related to my certificate as a dietitian. Montreal General Hospital had an opening. They considered the courses I had taken in my training and, because I hadn't had enough chemistry, they decided I was not qualified for a position as a full dietitian. I was hired as an assistant.

I found an apartment with Brigitte, a German woman I had met at the hospital. It was a tiny apartment that we could barely afford, and we discovered after we moved in that it was infested with rats. I would watch them at night parading along the fence outside our window. They would clatter around in the trash cans, and sometimes even come into our apartment looking for food.

Brigitte was difficult to live with. She was always afraid that someone was going to catch her. Sometimes she would turn on me, accusing me of things she only imagined. I would say to her, "No, Brigitte, I didn't do that. I am fine. Nothing is wrong with me."

I made friends with my coworkers at the hospital. There were times at lunch when I would be sitting at a table with Americans, British, French, and Canadians. I wondered, "If these people were so nice, why had their countries been the enemies of Germany during the war?"

I saw them at meals with a hand on their laps under the table. In Germany, the polite way was to keep your hands visible at all times. I wondered how they could eat if their hands were not above the table.

I also discovered that my custom of going from person to person to introduce myself and shake everyone's hand was not considered good manners. I was told to just greet the whole group at once. "Hi, how is everyone?" would be sufficient, even when meeting a new group of people. It felt so impolite not to greet each person.

I got to know a German doctor who was finishing his schooling and working at the hospital. He invited me out for coffee one day, and on another, he planned a picnic in the Laurentians, the mountains north of the city. He would call me over the loudspeaker at work, "Fraülein Merkel, please come to the phone." My supervisor said, "Tell him to stop calling you and interrupting your work."

Then Vati called me. He said, "I need to ask you something. Do you know a German doctor who says he works with you?"

I found out that he had looked up Vati and flown to Paris where Vati was now working with NATO. Vati had invited him to dinner at the restaurant at the NATO center. Over dinner, the doctor had asked for my hand in marriage. Vati's answer was that he would talk with me.

I was appalled. "I barely know him. How can I say yes?"

Questions and Answers

My job at the hospital was to go to patients' rooms to help them decide what they would like to eat. I began to notice that some of the patients had numbers tattooed on their forearms. I asked one of my coworkers what this was. She explained that these were Jews who had been in the concentration camps during the war. I knew nothing about these camps. I asked more questions and began to hear about the horrible things that we Germans had done. The descriptions sickened me. I began to see myself the way they must see me.

The new information about my people began to trouble me even when I was not at work. One night when I couldn't sleep, I wandered in the streets. I thought that if I could find a pastor, maybe he would be able to help. I saw a church that was dark, but the house next to it was brightly lit. In Germany, the pastor always lived next door to the church, and I decided this must be the pastor's home. I rang the bell. An old woman answered the door. She saw my distress and invited me in. She and her sister were already in their pajamas with fine beaded hairnets keeping their hair in place for the night. They settled me at the kitchen table and offered me tea. I cried as I explained my loneliness and my emptiness. I discovered that they had nothing to do with the church next door and that they were Jewish. I was suddenly afraid that they were going to hate me because I was German. Instead, one of them put her arm around me and told me that God had heard my cries and that He would take care of me. They suggested that I speak with their rabbi. They had to explain that a rabbi was the leader of a synagogue. I knew that would not be wise – he would probably hate me and even want to kill me for what my people had done. When I left, I felt greatly comforted, even though I still had no answers.

I was struggling with the languages. I had learned English and French in school, but that had been years ago and neither language was easy for me. I had a few mix-ups at work. When the head dietitian went on vacation, she put me in charge of the sixteenth floor. One of the doctors ordered two pancakes. I passed his order on as two panties. Everyone laughed. They had to explain what I had said. I laughed with them but decided that I needed to learn the language better.

I enrolled in an English class at McGill University. The professor learned of my desire to find a church. He recommended Cote des Neiges Presbyterian Church. I went to some services and was delighted with the warm, personal atmosphere. I discovered that the church also met the Lehmann's criteria – that Jesus Christ was the center of all their activities and that the preaching was based on the Bible.

After I started studying, my friend Zena invited me to a Bible study. Her plan was not intended just to help me with my English but to further my understanding of the Christian faith. I agreed to go with the thought of it being a friendly atmosphere for my English practice.

In spite of my English classes, the patients at the hospital heard my accent and often asked where I was from. As I heard more of what had happened during the war, I was ashamed to admit I was German. I wanted to say I was from Sweden, but then I was more afraid of lying. One time, after I said I was from Germany, a patient responded saying, "For a German, you are quite nice." Another patient turned away and mumbled something about being SS. I had to ask what that meant. I began to hear little snippets of their lives. "My sister was in Auschwitz..."

A friend, Carmen Woodrow, took me aside and explained about Hitler's plan to eliminate all Jews. My teachers in Poland had taught us the glory of our country and strict obedience to all that Hitler decreed. The songs, the marching, the punishments, the fear – they all began to roll around in my mind.

I thought about how I grew up. Omi always talked about Hitler and his wonderful plan to rule the world. I remembered the warm feeling I got when people said that Hitler would take care of us.

When the bombing was bad in Berlin, Hitler had moved us to Poland, and I remembered what a good time I had in our years there. It had been the happiest time of my childhood. But there were Polish children who, according to Hitler, were subhuman, and they were not to be our playmates. I had not liked being told that we shouldn't play with them, but I did not question the reasoning. I began to see that this was a Nazi teaching and was not true. Then I wondered about whose houses we had been living in. Who were the people who served us? What were their lives like before the war?

I asked about Hitler's plan to settle his new lands with his German Aryan people. My family, with our Estonian heritage, fit his image of perfection. I started to see my blond hair and blue eyes as a curse.

The only thing I had known about Jews was that they were dirty, unruly, nasty people that we should not care about. They were only evil. I remembered the ragged little boy begging on the street of the village. Gisela had hurried me away and would not answer my questions. She only said that he was a Jew.

I heard about the concentration camps. I learned about the cattle cars carrying the Jews from their homes to the camps. It came flooding back that I had seen one of these trains. I had wondered about the scared faces and the flailing arms I had seen through the grated windows of the cars.

I thought of my uncles. Onkel Hans always wore his uniform. Where did he go when he wasn't at home? What was his position in the Reich? Onkel Biller, too. He was not as mean as Onkel Hans, but he also had a uniform and would often be away from home.

The thoughts of all I had seen and all I had been taught rolled around in my head. I became angry with my mother, my father, my aunts, uncles, grandmother, and all of my teachers. No one would answer my questions. I now understood why they all were hiding the truth. I didn't know if they felt guilty about their beliefs, but I could not forgive them.

I felt my guilt of being a part of Hitler's plan. I did not choose my place in it, but my family and my whole culture was to blame. The weight of this shame haunted me. It was unbearable. I did not want to live anymore.

One night, I was in my room struggling with these thoughts. It came into my mind that I should pray. I knelt down beside my bed and asked God that, if Jesus is really the Savior, could He set me free from this guilt? I begged Him to help me.

As I got up from my knees, I felt peace flooding my soul. He had heard me. I knew I was cleansed and forgiven. I knew I had been set free. I felt like a turtle whose shell had just fallen off. Without thinking, I switched on the radio. A Billy Graham Crusade was being broadcast, and I heard them singing, "God Will Take Care of You." My heart was filled up with joy.

In the morning, I couldn't wait to share my new life. I ran to the home of some friends I knew from church. Even though it was only 6:00 a.m., they came to the door.

"I'm saved! I'm saved!" They hugged me and said how pleased they were that I was their new sister in Christ.

In the days following, I developed a thirst to know more about the Jews. My friend Carmen had said that they were in the Bible, that the Old Testament told their story. I started reading in Genesis.

When I got into Exodus and was reading about Moses and the plagues in Egypt, the weather outside my room changed. Hailstones started to hit my window. I realized that God was powerful enough to cause the plagues. Now He saw me reading this story and chose to show me His power with this hailstorm at just the right time!

It was as if someone had removed scales from my eyes. I saw how much the Lord cares about the Jewish people. His love for His people began to grow in my heart as well. I wanted to tell everyone about the joy I had found in His forgiveness.

I carried a little Bible in the pocket of my uniform and every chance I got I would take it out. One of the doctors asked me what I was always reading. When he heard my answer, he said, "Whaaaat? The Bible?"

I responded, "You should get your own Bible. It's the best book I've ever read." His reaction didn't matter to me. I was so hungry for the Word that I couldn't put it down.

Not only did I have a love for the Jewish people, but there was a woman at church who was severely deformed. Instead of turning away from her as I had been taught, I was able to embrace her and tell her that I love her.

41

Jutta

June 1961

In the Laurentian Mountains

Retreat

THE SERMONS at church started to make even more sense. I wanted to learn more, and I was eager for friends who had also put their faith in Jesus. I began to attend the Young Peoples' Fellowship.

Derek was one of the men in the group. He invited me to attend a retreat that Scripture Union was planning for a weekend. He said that it would be a time of fun and studying the Bible. It would be in a village in the Laurentians. The idea of getting away from the city sounded wonderful as well.

I was scheduled to work that weekend. I asked the head dietitian if I could change my schedule. At first, she said no. Then she decided that if we could find a substitute, I could go. I told the Lord that if it is His will, then I will go. I looked around and found someone to work for me. The head dietitian approved. Derek was very happy when I told him I could come.

The retreat was in a beautiful setting. The buildings were set in a meadow filled with wildflowers, and it was on the shore of a small lake.

The lectures were given by a man from Switzerland. He spoke English, but it must have been worse than mine. I had trouble following until my friend Helen helped. She "translated" what he was saying into better English.

Between the lectures I made friends with some little girls who lived in the area as they played in the meadow. I sat down and wove them crowns with the daisies growing there, the way I knew from my life in Austria.

While I was working, a young man came up and asked my name and introduced himself. I answered in my best English, but my accent must have given me away because he immediately switched to German. I was amazed to hear him speak my language so well. He sat on the grass and watched while I made the crowns. When we went back to the next lecture, he offered to sit with me and translate whatever I could not understand. It felt so good to have someone explain the teaching in my language.

He stayed next to me for the rest of the weekend. This man was good-looking, warm, and natural. We went for walks, and when the teacher told us to share our thoughts with someone, we sat under a big maple tree and talked.

We spent the recreation times with our other friends. He was a show-off when it came to the swimming time. He made sure I was watching before he took an elegant dive. He was fun to be with and seemed to love the Lord, a new essential for any good friends. I enjoyed my time with him. It meant a lot that he was recently from Europe. I felt there was a lot we had in common because of that connection.

At the end of the weekend, he asked me to ride back to Montreal with him in his fancy car. Another girl wanted to ride with him as well, but he seemed happy when she got a ride with someone else.

When he dropped me off at my apartment, he asked if he could see me again. I said yes.

42
Tom
June 1961
In the Laurentian Mountains

Retreat

ONE AFTERNOON, Mother had a few ladies from the church over for coffee. As I was fleeing to a tennis game, one of them asked me if I had anything planned for an upcoming weekend. She suggested I consider going to a youth retreat organized by Scripture Union, an organization which published Bible study guides and encouraged young people to engage in daily Bible reading.

She slyly added, "Tom, you may be interested to know that a girl who I think is cut out for you will be there!"

"You bet your life I will be there," was my instant response. Could this be the signal I was waiting for? Wow!

That night I called my friend Derek and told him about the weekend idea. "Derek, you and I have had good times together in the youth group and at our dinners together. I know that both of us could make these times even more enjoyable if each of us found a nice girl. How about coming along with me?"

Derek was equally responsive.

That night, I gratefully congratulated the Lord for this sign of His apparently quick action.

Friday afternoon, Derek and I took off in my shiny convertible and arrived at Val Morin in the Laurentians as the sun was sliding toward the horizon.

As we dropped our bags in the barn, which housed the guys, I looked through the window and saw a lovely girl fashioning a wreath of daisies. The perfect evening, beautiful scenery, and this charming activity, which I had not seen since I had left Hungary, filled me with delight. I walked over and introduced myself. When she looked at me with her lovely eyes and told me her name, I knew immediately that she was from Europe. I thought she was Swedish, but it turned out that she was a newcomer from Germany.

She continued making the wreath as a little girl watched with anticipation. I continued the conversation in German to her surprise and obvious pleasure. She had something unusually charming about her. I saw no reason to end the conversation after the wreath was completed and was placed on the little girl's head.

The supper bell rang, and I suggested that we sit together. She obliged. We had a good time with those around the table.

I followed her like a shadow – walking in the meadow, sitting under the big maple tree during sharing times, swimming in the pond. Her only escape was when she went back to her dorm where no men were allowed.

Derek followed the same strategy with Helen, an attractive girl who had arrived from England a few months before. When the retreat ended, we drove home as a foursome – looking forward to more of the same.

Back in my room, I went on my knees before even turning on the light. I thanked God for the girl he had put in my way. In fact, I thanked Him for the girl I felt would become my wife. I thought the match appeared so perfect it did not occur to me it takes two to make that decision.

I rushed to the phone to thank Mrs. Greer for her suggestion to attend the retreat.

"Audrey, your tip worked! She is exactly as you said – a girl cut out for me. I will pursue her with vigor!"

"Really? How come Chris did not mention a thing to me after she got home?"

"I am talking about Jutta, Audrey. Did you have Chris in mind for me? If so, I am sorry, but thanks anyway! I am sure Chris will find a better guy than me."

I had not realized that Chris was Audrey's tenant, and her plan was to hitch me up with her. Audrey was instrumental in me finding the one God had in mind for me.

43

Jutta

1961-1962

Montreal

Dating

SOON AFTER that, Tom invited me to dinner at The Troika, a fancy Russian restaurant. I was thinking, "Why not?"

I wore a beautiful dress Mutti had bought for me before I left. She had said that I may have a need for something dressy. It was a pale yellowish-beige with a touch of orange roses on it. It had short, puffy sleeves with a tender green ribbon made into a bow and a pleated skirt. I felt beautiful when I wore it.

He picked me up in the fancy '57 Chevy and held the door for me as I got in. I decided that he must like me if he was willing to spend so much money at a classy restaurant.

I liked him very much until he asked me to use the informal way of addressing him. This meant using "du" instead of "Sie." In Germany, "du" was only used for close friends or family members. With a man, it meant you were close enough to be engaged. I was shocked and didn't answer.

I told my roommate about his question. I decided that this was too pushy. I would not go out with him again. She agreed that I should end the relationship.

I talked to another friend who asked me if I liked him. I said yes, but wasn't sure now.

Then Tom called for another date, and I found myself saying yes.

He invited me to go with him to the movies. "Exodus" was playing. It was about the struggle for Jews to settle in Palestine in 1948. It warmed my heart to learn more about the Jewish people and their history.

There were other dates as well, but the most important one ended with a walk on Mount Royal. We were admiring the view of the river and the ships when Tom turned to me with a serious look in his eyes.

He said, "I really like you a lot, but there's something I need to tell you."

I thought, "Oh no. What's coming now? He has a disease or something."

"I'm Jewish."

"Oh, you're Jewish?" I was so relieved that I started laughing.

"Why are you laughing?"

"Well, you are Jewish. I am Gentile. I think it is wonderful."

Tom seemed to be very pleased with my answer. I thought that God had a wonderful sense of humor. He had prepared me for this moment through all my study of the Bible.

My willingness to trust Tom inspired him to find creative ways for us to spend our time together. We enjoyed exploring Montreal, taking in the colorful sights in the daytime and watching the city at night from the top of Mount Royal or Westmount, going to classical concerts, and hiking in the Laurentians.

We seemed to enjoy the same activities, and we felt comfortable with each other whether we were alone or in the midst of fellowship with others. It was nice to have someone special with whom I could discuss the Bible and with whom I could share my thoughts.

We went with the Young Peoples' Fellowship on outings. One of our favorites was to Lake Champlain, where we had a picnic lunch and went swimming.

At some point in our dating, I told Tom about my background. He didn't seem to mind that I had grown up with the Nazi teaching and its attitude toward the Jews. He knew that I had changed and I now had God's love in my heart.

There was something in his character that drew me to him. He was everything I wanted in a future husband – always loving, always kind. He always opened doors for me. I thought, "Wow! He is really a gentleman." I was taken by him. He was always funny, but he didn't tell slippery jokes. He never looked down on others, and he put everyone at ease. He was natural and easy-going. He didn't fiddle around when he wanted to say something serious. I also liked that he spoke fluent German.

Once when he was picking me up for a date, I saw him come toward me, and it was like a thunderstorm went through my body. I knew then that my feelings were brewing into a very good cake!

New Job

I became overwhelmed by the stress of the job at the hospital, and I heard about a position at a school for Native American children teaching "Home and Industry." Part of my coursework at the Frauenfachschule had been in home economics. That would come in handy for this job. I was offered the position, and I gladly accepted.

My responsibilities included teaching leather crafts, basket weaving, sewing, wood carving, and enamel work. We made wooden boxes; shoe polishers out of wood and lamb's wool; and forks, knives, and spoons carved out of bamboo. I taught the students how to use an electric table saw, to shellac a piece of wood, to make brooches and other jewelry out of copper and to fire them in a little kiln, and how to sew with a sewing machine. It was a nice change from the stress of the hospital.

44
Tom
1961-1962
Montreal

Dating

JUTTA AND I kept getting together. We spoke to one another in German, but after my having spoken English for years, the formal you, "Sie," felt a bit unnatural. I suggested we change to the informal "du," which in Germany was reserved for close relationships and often held back until engagement.

Jutta had not made a full transition from the formal world of Europe to the freer, modern life of Canada, so she was taken aback by my bold approach. Her German roommate suggested she escape the relationship or at least be extremely cautious. Fortunately, her concerns faded as we kept seeing each other. Little did I know how close I was to being let go!

Mother must have noticed I was both happier and more pensive, but she made no remarks. All she cared about was my closer walk with God. I felt it was too early to stir the pot and introduce the likelihood of another relationship entering her life.

Jutta and I had good times together in the Young Peoples' Fellowship, nice walks and drives together, and fun attending concerts and movies. Probably the best thing in our relationship was that we were always comfortable with each other no matter whether something happened or was said, or not. Our tastes and interests matched, and we met more and more frequently and for longer periods. I loved watching Jutta's graceful movements and listening to her gentle voice. I loved everything about her! In fact, I found Jutta unique in so many ways that I knew she was God's perfect complement for me.

Jewish

With Jutta's background of having been raised in Nazi Germany, there was a hurdle we needed to overcome – her reaction to my Jewish background.

I invited her for dinner at Balalaika, an elegant Russian restaurant in downtown Montreal. While we awaited the entree, I casually asked her if she saw any problem in my being a Jew.

"Are you serious? What a delightful surprise! God has a great sense of humor!" She chuckled so sweetly that I felt like getting up to give her a kiss on the cheek. It took strong willpower to restrain myself.

"This is terrific!" she exclaimed. "I never dreamed of dating someone belonging to the people of God's covenant through Abraham. The beauty of our relationship is a fulfillment of God's plan for His Church – Jew and Gentile made one through faith in the Messiah of Israel."

Her radiant faith had removed the trepidation of sharing this with her, but I wondered if she might be concerned about sharing this with her family. However, I knew that her father had spent most of the war not in Germany, but in Japan on a technical mission, and that after the war, he was chosen by the Allies to assist in establishing the new German military. It was unlikely the Allies would have employed him unless his records were acceptable.

Home Stretch

By the summer of 1962, there was no doubt in our minds that we were made for each other. We spent a week at Word of Life and made progress toward deciding on a lifetime commitment.

After we returned, I asked Jutta out one night for a walk near the top of Westmount, a popular romantic spot overlooking Montreal. The city's lights seemed to mirror the stars of the clear summer sky.

We sat down on a bench, and I asked the big question. Jutta did not keep me waiting long with the answer. A week later, we announced our engagement and started preparations for a life together.

The first step was to move Jutta closer to where I lived so we could see each other every day. After a short search in the neighborhood, I found a nice apartment for her and her friend Joy across the street from mine.

One Saturday, the two girls got ready, and I moved them with the help of a rented truck. We had things organized so well that we could have returned the truck within two hours. Driving it, however, was so much fun that I drove it around town for another hour, in and out of heavy traffic, before I returned it. It was the beginning of my love affair with trucks.

During the next months, we walked cheerfully toward the altar without any doubts or fears. We met every night at least for a little chat and prayer together. Through this closeness and God's strong presence in our relationship, we felt that our time of preparation for the marriage was completely in His hands. We openly shared our weaknesses in order to avoid disappointments after the Big Day. We had a great sense of peace, joy, and abundant assurance of having made the right choice.

Mother could sense my mind was made up and was wise enough not to interfere. Jutta's mother appeared to find it a bit harder to overcome the cultural barriers. I used my fairly good German to warm her heart during her talks with Jutta on the telephone.

45

Jutta

Summer 1962

Schroon Lake, New York

Montreal, Canada

Decision

Word of Life Camp

AFTER WE had been dating for a while, Tom decided that we should go to the Word of Life camp where he had reconnected with the Lord. He thought that getting away for a week would be fun and would be a good time for us to consider our relationship.

I had talked about Tom with my roommate before we went. She said that he is a nice guy and asked if I was serious about him. I thought about all of the good things about him. The Lehmanns had told me that a test for someone you're considering marrying would be thinking about whether he would make a good father to your children. I realized that Tom would be a wonderful father.

While we were there, I had time to think about what marrying Tom would mean. I would have to give up the idea of returning to Europe. That was hard. Did I want to make a home on this continent? Then I thought about the peace I had when I was with him.

There were fun times during the week. For one of the evenings, we had to come to supper with some sort of creative hat. I took on the challenge to make a hat for Tom to wear. I picked orange and blue flowers and some greens in the surrounding meadows. I wove them together and then added a feather I had found. I hung keys on the sides to look like earrings. It looked crazy, but he won the prize!

One of the other attendees was a guy from California. He was in the Air Force. He made it very clear that he wanted me to sit next to him. I was thankful that Tom told him that the chair next to him was for me. The Air Force guy understood. Then Tom asked me to move closer so that no one could snatch me away!

I continued to think about the future with Tom after we returned to Montreal. I prayed that the Lord would show me definitely what I should do. He answered my prayer and made it clear to me that I should marry Tom and not move back to Europe.

Proposal

Our dates were often for dinner at nice restaurants, but we usually ended with a walk on Mount Royal. On one of those dates, we sat on a bench in the park near the top. Tom turned to me and asked if I would marry him. He had always said that he wouldn't kiss me until we were engaged. All of a sudden it was just natural to say yes.

He kissed me then.

Everyone in the youth group said, "Oh, he is a great person. Did he ask you to marry him yet?"

"Yes, he did."

"I hope you said yes."

We had to call my parents. I was a little nervous. Mutti answered the phone.

"Are you sitting down?" I asked. "I am engaged."

"Who's the lucky guy?" she asked.

"His name is Tom." I took a deep breath. "He is from Hungary, and he is Jewish."

"Does it, of all people, HAVE to be a Jew?"

Walter happened to be visiting that day so he heard the news from the same phone call.

After more talking, Mutti, Vati, and Walter decided, "If this is your choice, we trust that you are making the right decision even if you never come back to Germany."

Tom's mother was not happy that he was going to marry a German. She told me, "For a German girl, you are quite nice." Her Hungarian friends from work also didn't like that her son was going to marry a German.

Tom and I had total peace about our future together. We considered our different backgrounds to be a blessing, not a problem.

Tom decided that we needed to live closer to each other. He found an apartment across the street from his. He came over every evening after that.

We read the Bible and a Scripture Union devotional and prayed together. In one of the passages in the devotional, we read from Ecclesiastes 4:9-10: "Two are better than one because they have a good return for their labor. If either of them falls down, one can help the other up." We felt this confirmed our decision.

My love for Tom blossomed during the time of waiting for the wedding. When he came over for our devotions, he always took off his boots and put on slippers. I thought that was so thoughtful.

I felt like everything in me was saying, "Yes!"

Tom asked me why I was so timid, like a flower on the wall. But after he asked me to marry him, somehow my shyness went away. He had the gift of God to bring me out.

"You are so quiet." He said it in a very loving way. "I want you to come out of your shell. How can I help you?"

At a beach near Montreal, I found a fisherman's net. I made a cozy corner in my room with a star hanging on the wall. Tom liked it because it was the image of the net he caught me in.

46
Tom
1962-1963
Montreal

Preparations

We agreed that what we were about to do was to embark on a lifetime voyage together with the purpose of pleasing the One who made us. With this purpose, we also hoped that He would allow us to enjoy each other and life to the fullest, and that included having fun.

We decided the wedding day would be our day, with the Lord presiding, the minister officiating, and our friends and the two mothers looking on. We had no intention of impressing anyone, expending great effort on organizing a perfect wedding, and spending a lot of money that neither of us had. We refused to succumb to the all-too-popular premarital hassle which replaces the joy and peace so desirable before making the big step into a life long relationship. We had a beautiful time, without any stress, enjoying each other under the guidance of our Lord.

The reception was to be held in the fellowship hall of the church. The ladies in the church had offered to prepare a buffet-style meal. The only thing we had to decide was what types of beverages to provide.

We asked our former pastor, Reverend Hector MacRury, if he would officiate. He obliged graciously. His willingness to drive eight hours from his new home in Toronto expressed his interest in our lives.

As for the wedding itself, we invited about eighty people. We hoped sincerely that they would enjoy the occasion and see and feel God's presence. We made no effort to make it perfect. We were not worried about a bridesmaid dropping her flowers or an usher making an awkward step.

The Night Before

The night before, Jutta stayed in the Sheraton Hotel downtown with her mother. Mutti had arrived a few days earlier from Germany. Her family wanted her to have a final chance to check out the fellow Jutta planned to marry, and, barring drastically worrisome findings, to help Jutta get ready for the occasion and witness the "loss" of her fourth child.

I must have succeeded in behaving well enough to quell her fears and win her approval. She enjoyed meeting Mother and our circle of friends and did everything to help Jutta and the team in charge of the preparations to make our wedding beautiful.

Following the rehearsal dinner, I walked over to Mother's new home, a nice little flat we had found for her down the street. We had a memorable tea, talking about the times we went through together in Hungary and the few years since she had come to Canada.

She was a brave trooper, hiding her concerns about continuing life alone in her new country. She reassured me by telling me of the care she sensed from her friends in the church and by a few elderly Hungarian ladies with whom she met weekly for coffee and a game of rummy. I was touched by her prayer of grateful surrender to God's will and by her assurance that our marriage would become a blessing to all, including her.

After a warm hug, I left her for a walk around the block in the starry, spring night, reflecting on what was about to happen. I could not help being grateful for how it seemed God had led me from the day I escaped from Hungary, through the journey to Canada, and to this night before marrying the woman He had chosen for me.

A great peace flooded my heart when I turned off the light and listened to the gentle ticking of my alarm clock.

47
Jutta
April 1963
Montreal

Wedding

THE DAY couldn't come fast enough.

We decided that we would not let concerns about the wedding rob us from enjoying every day. During those weeks and months, I had the opportunity to explain about the Jewish roots of Christian faith to my friends and family. I began to understand that I would be called to tell of God's love to the Jewish people. God was also calling me to bring this message to Christians.

Mutti came for the wedding. I don't know if Vati didn't want to come or if it was true when he said that he didn't have the money for the two of them to come. Instead of coming, he sent me forty-eight gorgeous roses.

When we picked up Mutti at the airport and she met Tom, she took me aside and said, "You can marry him. He is very nice."

I answered, "Even if you hadn't liked him, I would marry him anyway!"

Mutti and I stayed at the Sheraton Hotel in downtown Montreal the night before the wedding. A friend of mine made the wedding dress and veil. It was a simple design but just right.

When I came down the stairs in the hotel, it was like a fairy tale. I had the veil on. I felt like a queen. Everyone in the lobby clapped for me. I heard comments, "Oh my goodness, she is gorgeous."

It was a stormy day, very windy and SO cold. I had to hold my veil on or the wind would have pulled it off.

Don, an elder at the church, picked us up at the hotel. When we got to the church, we couldn't find anywhere to park. It turned out that, although we had only invited twenty-five people, everyone else in the church and our other friends decided that we forgot to invite them so they came, too. There were 125 people waiting for us while we searched for a parking space.

48

Tom

April 27, 1963

Montreal

The Day

SATURDAY, APRIL 27, 1963, was a beautiful, sunny, spring day. I got up a little earlier than usual. No matter how we tried to sail into this day smoothly, it was still to be the greatest day of my life.

After getting on my knees to talk with God, I had a good breakfast, got dressed, and went down to inspect my car, already packed for the honeymoon. Even though I had washed it the night before, I noticed it could use some final touches. I got a bucket and a wet rag and, dressed in my wedding suit, cufflinks and all, I gave it a careful last cleaning. I picked up Mother, and we drove to Cotes des Neiges Presbyterian Church.

As I stood at the altar at 10:00 a.m. sharp waiting for my beloved, Reverend MacRury whispered, "You rascal, you said maybe we would fill half the church. Look! There is hardly a seat left."

"Sorry," I answered. "Everybody we invited came and a few others who it appears were sure we would miss if they did not come."

At 10:10, he asked, "Do you think Jutta will make it here?"

"She had better," I said. "I did not arrange for a substitute. Don't worry, Rev, she is usually..."

At that moment, Reverend Mac winked at me with a broad smile as the organ indicated the arrival of the bride.

I could not help but turn back to glance at Jutta. She looked beautiful!

As she walked to the front following her bridesmaids, Joy, Helen, and Brenda, the solemnity of the moment filled me with a deep joy.

Don gave Jutta away in the absence of her father.

The ceremony was brief and beautiful. We sang a hymn together with the congregation. Then Jutta's First Nations home economic students sang the song, "The Love of God is Greater Still." Reverend Mac gave a short homily, and we exchanged our vows and wedding rings. When it came to kissing the bride, I could not help but wink at the congregation first to their roaring delight.

A friend of mine planned to record the memorable day with his movie camera for us to cherish. The camera kept clicking away. We discovered later that the film was stuck on the first frame.

The lunch in the church basement was a relaxed, happy event. We managed to talk with everybody but had little to eat ourselves. Someone began to play the piano and soon the hall was filled with cheerful music and songs. We chose this time to slip away from the crowd.

When we stepped out of the church, I looked at Jutta and suddenly realized that we should have arranged to have a professional photograph taken of us. We got into the Chevy and drove down to Mountain Street to the shop of a famous Hungarian photographer. When we entered in full wedding attire, his wife exclaimed in embarrassment, “How could my husband have forgotten this?”

“He did not forget, Madam,” I said. “He doesn't know about it. We did this on the spur of the moment. I hope we are able to get a photo.”

The maestro nearly dropped his brown bag lunch on seeing us. He had the same embarrassed and guilty look on his face until we explained the situation.

. “Well, now that you are here,” he said, “we might as well get the job done!”

The picture turned out well enough that it served as the window display in his shop for several months. It became a treasured item for us and the only formal record of our day.

Little did we know that while we made the detour to the photographer, a whole squad of my colleagues was waiting near our home to “decorate” the car for our honeymoon. The president of my company, as I found out later, had spent the previous evening punching holes in empty cans and tying ropes onto them so that he could attach them to the back of my car to create a racket as we drove away. Others had worked on signs, and several waited to grease and spray my freshly washed, elegant convertible. Fortunately, we kept them waiting long enough that they finally dispersed in defeat.

When we returned to Mother's flat, we were ravenously hungry. She served us lunch at her kitchen table, the two of us in full wedding regalia. Jutta looked so beautiful, I asked her to keep her wedding gown on for the rest of the day, and I wore my wedding suit. That is how we travelled to our honeymoon destination, husband and wife.

We left around 3:00 p.m. for a one-week trip through the Adirondacks and a good part of New England.

49

Tom

April 27 – May 5, 1963

New York, New England, and Back to Montreal

Honeymoon

As we cruised toward the Canadian/U.S. border, people passing us noticed Jutta's unusual attire. They honked their horns and waved with smiles. We got quite a concert of horns when I stopped the car on the shoulder of the road to take a picture of Jutta wearing her wedding gown with the car as background. It was a happy feeling to be celebrated by strangers. We kept looking at our wedding rings and getting used to how they felt on our fingers.

When we got to the border, the customs and immigration officials wanted to have Jutta get out of the car and sign the entry book in the office. I talked them into bringing the book out to the car so she could sign it without having to get out. The entire staff came out of the office, smiling at the strange phenomenon – Jutta with wedding veil and dress signing the log through the car window.

It was getting dark when we got to the foot of Whiteface Mountain. I have always had picky taste about the places I liked to stay. Advertisements and brochures often disappointed me when I arrived at the real thing.

Consequently, we had decided not to make reservations and rather spend a little time searching for the right spot at the expense of not knowing where we would find one. Jutta got a high score from me by showing full trust that we would eventually end up at a good spot. Spontaneity has its risks but also its rewards.

A charming chalet that had been made into an inn, caught our eye. It was a bit off the road behind a patch of pine trees. There was a single window lit in the darkness. I left Jutta in the car while I inquired about a room. As it turned out, the inn was closed for the season. However, the owner noticed the carnation on my jacket, the dark suit, and an unusually sad look in my eyes. I was always good at looking sad when it served a useful purpose.

"Don't tell me you are newlyweds!" he said.

"We sure are, sir, and we believe in picking delightful places on the spot. Yours is just the kind of place we were looking for. In fact, the first one that caught our eye."

"Hey, Sally," he yelled, "come on down, look what we have here!" He turned to me. "Why don't you bring your bride in?"

I walked back to the car and helped Jutta along the path to the house. The owner and his wife watched through the door as the snow-white fairy and her groom emerged from the darkness. By the time we arrived at the door, the lady's tears were rolling down as she and her husband smiled at us.

"George, doesn't she remind you of me on our wedding day thirty years ago? Isn't she beautiful?"

The husband nodded and opened the door.

"We won't let you go any further this late in the evening. Come on in. We will turn on the heat. You can stay with us at least for the weekend."

We thanked them, and Jutta settled in our room while I got our two suitcases from the car.

It didn't take long before the room was warm and comfortable. Still in her wedding gown, Jutta went outside, picked some moss and proceeded to convert an ashtray into a nice green planter, giving me a taste of her knack for making any environment "gemütlich," a difficult-to-translate German word meaning more than "cozy."

We turned the light off after the best day in our young lives and praised the One who brought us to this experience in a way we could never have planned. If this day was an indication of the years to come, we thought we would have a colorful life ahead.

The next morning, we looked for an evangelical church nearby. What we did not realize was that that morning had been the time to switch to daylight savings. Thus, after a short breakfast, we pulled up to the church only to see people leaving. Fortunately, they knew about another church a mile away which held services an hour later. We hopped in the car and made it in time.

I was hoping for a lovely message, a little special encouragement from the Lord on this very first Sunday in our married life. Instead we got a hellfire and brimstone barrage, which left us just about demolished. I had nothing against a reminder about my sinfulness, but to hear nothing but the dark side of my relationship to God was not really what I was longing for on the first day of our honeymoon.

We walked out of the little church somewhat discouraged. I put my arm around Jutta and told her it was good that at least the sun was shining. She thought the sermon was good, that the man had spoken the truth. I was not about to start a discussion on the subject. I was a happy groom walking in the sun with his bride.

As we walked a bit farther to stretch our legs and get some fresh air, we came to a bridge over a little river. I noticed that the flower decorating Jutta's jacket as well as my carnation, which we had placed in water overnight was, nevertheless, wilting. Jutta took the flowers and was about to throw them away when I caught her hand.

"How could you just throw these precious things in the dust? Why don't we walk to the middle of the bridge and let both of them float away in the cool water?"

They landed about fifteen feet apart. There must have been currents under the wooden bridge, because neither Jutta's flower nor mine moved. They just turned around slowly, and then to our amazement, started to float toward each other. We could hardly believe our eyes when we saw them touch each other in the center of the stream and only then float away together. We watched them, holding hands, and when they disappeared in the distance, still in the center of the stream, we turned to each other. I could not help but embrace her after this delightful scene.

A cheerful lunch followed, and by the time we got back to the chalet, the angry country preacher's words had faded from my memory.

The rest of our honeymoon was just as good as its beginning at the lovely inn. Because we were their only guests, the owners pampered us as if we were their own. They made us royal breakfasts. We played tag in the huge dining hall, and we hiked Whiteface Mountain. It was warm enough that a shirt sufficed even though there was still snow. Our hosts sent us off with a bag of food and warm hugs.

One day, we had breakfast served in the nicest room in the elegant Somerset Hotel in Boston. The next day, our supper was a roast beef sandwich in a dubious-looking hole-in-the-wall eatery. We enjoyed the variety.

I got sunburned on Old Orchard Beach in Maine. Jutta covered my back with yogurt to take away the heat of the burn.

We stayed at the lovely Edelweiss Inn in New Hampshire and rode through Vermont with the top of the convertible down. We enjoyed every minute together.

The only moment of tension was when Jutta asked me to stop for an ice cream cone. I was glad to oblige but refrained from getting one for myself.

"Are you sure you would not like one?" she asked.

"Not really," I said. "Just let me have a single lick." The emphasis was on "single" without committing to size.

Emboldened by our loving relationship, I was sure she wanted me to savor the moment and took a fair-sized bite of her ice cream.

"Wow! You sure took a good chunk, my dear knight! Next time I will be a little less generous!"

In the decades since, Jutta has reminded me of this experience when I have naively approached her with a similar request!

We arrived home on Sunday just in time for the evening church service. We were surrounded by our friends who could see immediately what this superb week had done for us.

We settled in our new home and our first activity was to open our wedding gifts. Our friends had coordinated well, and we received not even one duplicate item.

Jutta returned to her job, and I turned into an engineer again the next morning. It took us a long time before we stopped talking about all the fun and joy we had had in the first week of our marriage.

Tom – April 27-May 5, 1963

The joy God has given us for fifty-four years is evidence of His care through all of our lives – preserving us through the harrowing experiences of our childhoods, bringing us to faith in His son Jesus, and drawing us together in marriage.

50

Author's Epilogue

April 1963 – January 2018

Montreal, Canada

Arlington, Massachusetts

Wayland, Massachusetts

Nine months after the wedding, Tom and Jutta's first daughter, Esther, was born, and two years later, Maria was added to the family.

Soon after Maria's birth, Tom's job was terminated as the company closed its doors. Along with his severance pay, he received invitations to interview at two of the company's competitors. He was offered a job at EG&G in Boston, Massachusetts.

They rented an apartment in Arlington. Their third daughter, Rebecca, was born while they were living there. A few years later, they were able to buy a house on a quiet street in Wayland, a comfortable town west of the city.

They found fellowship and Jesus-centered, Bible-based teaching at Park Street Church in downtown Boston. Tom served as an Elder for many years, and they led Bible studies in their home. They told their story to anyone who would listen in the hope that all would know of the Lord's love, His power for reconciliation, and His call to salvation. They were invited to speak to church groups, Jewish gatherings, on university campuses, and on a national radio program.

After a few years with EG&G, Tom had the opportunity to found his own company that made equipment for precise temperature testing of semiconductor wafers, printed circuit boards, and other components used in the computer industry. He was president of the company, Temptronic, until he retired in 1999.

He traveled for business throughout his career. He was finally able to tour Britain, as well as Europe, Israel, India, and East Asia. He introduced his daughters to the joys of travel as he included the family on many of the trips.

Tom tells a story about crossing the English Channel on his way to Belgium:

I got the truck parked, put on a warm jacket, and went up to the deck for another glance at the cliffs of Dover. Then the horn blew, and the ferry left the shore. I walked to the bow remembering the time in 1956 when I said farewell to Europe. I stood at the rail thinking with gratitude about how God led me – a twenty-four-year-old, stateless bachelor with everything I owned in an old briefcase – through so many experiences and uncertainties, to this promising trip back to the Old Country as a husband of a wonderful wife, a father of three delightful children, and a president of a business appreciated around the world.

Tom began battling Parkinson's Disease in 2006. He slowed the progress of its symptoms for ten years with walking, exercise, and staying active in all of his usual activities.

In December of 2016, after an accident precipitated by the Parkinson's symptoms and after lingering for a week – long enough to say goodbye to a multitude of friends – he passed into eternity surrounded by the family. The memorial service at Park Street Church three weeks later was attended by more than 400 friends and colleagues. A letter from one of his Boy Scout friends was one of the many remembrances that were shared. A few weeks after the service, the Boston Globe ran a special article on him. His life and the impact of his company in the Boston area made his passing relevant to many.

Jutta misses him terribly but knows God's timing is perfect. She is looking forward to the day when she will join Tom in the presence of the Lord Jesus.

January 2018

Where in Life Do You Stand?

The sun is setting fast.
Do not build your house on sand.
It will never last.

Jesus is calling you with a tender voice,
To come to Him
And make this choice.

The words in the Bible are always true.
Jesus died for me and you.

The love of Jesus for you and me
Can never be measured,
But it sets us free.

Jutta Gerendas

For photos and more stories:

www.TomandJuttaTheBook.com

Barbara W. Pless

Barbara's mother's childhood in Berlin, ending with her family's escape in 1939, has given her perspective on the years of Hitler's rise to power. That her mother and Jutta lived in Berlin in the same years made both stories come to life. Even though Berlin is far from Budapest, her family's experiences mirrored Tom's as the persecution of the Jews spread throughout Europe.

Her writing projects, some for her undergraduate degree at Earlham College, some for her studies at Gordon-Conwell Theological Seminary, and graduate work at Emerson College, included essays on all aspects of the arts. She has also written poetry, a screenplay, and stage plays.

It has been her joy to bring Tom and Jutta's story to a wide audience.

30725803R00222

Made in the USA
Middletown, DE
28 December 2018